Reiki and Karmic Healing: Releasing Patterns from Past Lives

REIKI WISDOM SERIES
Beyond the Symbols — The Path to True Mastery

Sacred Symbol of Reiki Wisdom

The sacred combination of the **circle, triangle, intersecting lines**, and **pentagram** represents the harmonious flow of spiritual and physical energy.

- The **circle** symbolizes **wholeness** and **spiritual protection**, reflecting the infinite and interconnected nature of Reiki energy.
- The **triangle** embodies **creation** and **balance**, representing the three pillars of Reiki — **mind, body, and spirit** — working in harmony.
- The **three converging lines** reflect **unity** and **focused intent**, directing energy flow through the chakras and meridians.
- The **pentagram** signifies **mastery of the elements** (earth, fire, water, air, and spirit) and the awakening of spiritual wisdom.

This symbol represents the manifestation of divine energy into physical reality through balance, alignment, and focused intention. It reflects the path to enlightenment — where mind, body, and spirit align to unlock deep healing and spiritual mastery.

Grand Master, Constance Santego

REIKI AND KARMIC HEALING: RELEASING PATTERNS FROM PAST LIVES

VOL. II OF THE REIKI WISDOM SERIES

Beyond the Symbols — The Path to True Mastery

Dr. Constance Santego

Maximillian Enterprises
Kelowna, BC

REIKI AND KARMIC HEALING
Copyright © 2025 by Dr. Constance Santego.

Copy Editor and Interior Design: Constance Santego
Book Layout: ©2017 BookDesignTemplates.com

Ordering Information:
Quantity sales. Special discounts are available on quantity purchases by corporations, associations, and others. For details, contact the address below.

Trade paperback ISBN: 978-1-990062-63-6
eBook ISBN 978-1-990062-64-3

Created and published In Canada. Printed and bound in the United States of America

First Edition
Published by Maximillian Enterprises
Kelowna, BC Canada
www.constancesantego.ca

Dedication

To the souls who have carried burdens across lifetimes, To the healers who walk between worlds, And to the lightworkers who dare to break generational cycles—

This book is for you.

May it serve as a guide, a mirror, and a remembrance. May your healing ripple across time, And may your freedom become your legacy.

"When you release the past with love, you reclaim your soul's truth. Through Reiki, you don't just heal— you remember who you are."
—Dr. Constance Santego

ALSO BY DR. CONSTANCE SANTEGO

NOVELS

Illegitimate Grace

Okanagan Trilogy:

Beneath the Vineyards
Under the Okanagan Sun
Guardian of the Lake

The Nine Spiritual Gifts Series:
Journey of a Soul – (Vol 1 Michael)
Language of a Soul – (Vol 2 Gabriel)
Prophecy of a Soul – (Vol 3 Bath Kol)
Healing of a Soul – (Vol 4 Raphael)
Miracles of a Soul – (Vol 5 Hamied)
Knowledge of a Soul – (Vol 6 Raziel)
Wisdom of a Soul – (Vol 7 Uriel)
Faith of a Soul – (Vol 8 Pistis Sophia)

NONFICTION
The Intuitive Life, The Gift Of Prophecy, Third Edition
Fairy Tales, Dreams And Reality... Where Are You On Your
Path? Second Edition
Your Persona... The Mask You Wear
Archangel Michael's Soul Retrieval Guide
Tesla And The Future Of Energy Medicine
Beyond Tesla: *Advancing The Science Of Energy Healing*
Tesla's Code: *Mastering Energy, Frequency, And Creative
Power*
Scaling Beyond 6 Figures: *Strategies for Health & Wellness
Professionals*

Beyond the Mind: *Harnessing the Power of Astral Projection for Creative Awakening*

Bend, Don't Break: *Finding Your Way Back to Abundance*
Ring Therapy: *A Guide to Healing and Balance*
Ring Therapy Pocket Guide
Floraopathy™: *The Art and Science of Vibrational Healing with Essential Oils*

REIKI WISDOM, SERIES:

Angelic Lifestyle, a Vibrant Lifestyle
Angelic Lifestyle 42-Day Energy Cleanse
Reiki and the Power of The Joint Points: *Unlocking Energy Pathways for Healing* (Vol I)

SECRETS OF A HEALER, SERIES:
Magic Of Aromatherapy (Vol I)
Magic Of Reflexology (Vol II)
Magic Of The Gifts (Vol III)
Magic Of Muscle Testing (Vol IV)
Magic Of Iridology (Vol V)
Magic Of Massage (Vol VI)
Magic Of Hypnotherapy (Vol VII)
Magic Of Reiki (Vol VIII)
Magic Of Advanced Aromatherapy (Vol IX)
Magic Of Esthetics (Vol X)
The Reiki Master's Manual (Vol XI)

ADULT COLORING JOURNALS

SERIES-ZEN COLORING:
Quantum Energy and Mindful Living Journal (Vol 1)
Reiki Energy Journal (Vol 2)
Nine Spiritual Gifts Journal (Vol 3)
I Forgive Journal (Vol 4)

FOR CHILDREN
I am Big Tonight. I Don't Need the Light

Contents

Preface

Reiki Wisdom:
Unlocking Energy Pathways for Healing

Healing Across Lifetimes: Releasing Karma, Ancestral Burdens, and Soul Contracts

Reiki has been the heartbeat of my healing practice since 1999. It has taken me through decades of transformation—not just in my own life but in the lives of the thousands I've taught, treated, and guided. Over time, I began to see a pattern: no matter how skilled or experienced someone was in energy healing, certain emotional or physical struggles persisted.

That's when I realized that some healing requires us to look **beyond this lifetime**.

Buried beneath chronic patterns, emotional loops, or unexplained fears are deeper layers of soul memory—contracts, beliefs, and trauma inherited from our ancestors or etched into us from past lives. These imprints don't just live in the mind or body; they shape our relationships, finances, health, purpose, and how we feel about being alive. They form the karmic web we're here to understand… and then transcend.

This book was born from that realization.

Reiki and Karmic Healing is a map into the unseen: the energetic threads of ancestry, soul contracts, and reincarnation that shape our path. But it is not just about awareness—it is about **release**. Through tools like my "I Forgives" method, BodyTalk-style tapping, past life regression, Reiki-infused soul work, and Akashic alignment techniques, you'll learn how to identify and unravel these patterns with clarity and compassion.

Whether you're a seasoned Reiki Master or a spiritual seeker exploring karmic healing for the first time, this book invites you to go deeper. Not just to heal—but to remember who you were… and **choose who you are becoming.**

You are not bound by the past.
You are the one who breaks the cycle.
You are the healer your lineage has been waiting for.

With gratitude, truth, and Reiki's eternal light,

Dr. Constance Santego
Grand Reiki Master

Note to Reader

A Word on Responsibility, Reiki, and Karmic Depth

Reiki is a gentle yet profound modality—one that supports healing on emotional, physical, spiritual, and energetic levels. It can help shift patterns held not only in the body and mind but within the soul's memory itself. However, Reiki is not a replacement for medical care or mental health treatment.

If you're navigating serious physical illness, trauma, or psychological distress, please consult a licensed healthcare professional. Just as you would see a doctor to set a broken bone, Reiki can assist in the healing process—but it does not take the place of conventional care. Instead, it works alongside it, calming the nervous system, balancing your energy field, and helping your body and soul reconnect with their natural rhythm of restoration.

This book explores the deeper realms of healing—territory that extends beyond symptoms and into the root causes held in karmic memory, ancestral lines, and spiritual contracts. These energetic imprints can carry across lifetimes, generations, and soul agreements. Through Reiki, these deeper patterns can be acknowledged, honored, and finally released. But energy work is not passive. Reiki invites you into a conscious relationship with your healing. It asks for your courage, your presence, and your commitment to growth.

This book includes:

- Spiritual and metaphysical frameworks
- Energy healing techniques
- The "I Forgives" method for emotional release
- Past life regression guidance
- Akashic journeywork and ancestral integration

Please use discernment and intuition as you move through the material. Not every technique is meant to be rushed. Healing is a spiral, not a straight line.

Important Guidelines:

- A **Level II Reiki certificate** (signed by a certified Reiki Master) is required if you plan to offer paid Reiki sessions to others.
- A **Level III (Reiki Master/Teacher) certificate** is required if you intend to teach Reiki or provide attunements.

This book is an offering to your soul—an invitation to return to the origin of your wounds so that you may also return to the **truth of who you are**. The deeper the healing, the greater your freedom.

You are your own healer.
Reiki is simply the light to guide you home.

With reverence and intention,
Dr. Constance Santego

Learning Outcome

Reiki and Karmic Healing: Releasing Patterns from Past Lives

This book is a transformative guide that weaves together traditional Reiki with advanced spiritual insight into **karma, ancestral imprinting, past life memory, soul contracts**, and emotional release. It bridges the worlds of energy medicine and soul work, helping you not only to **treat surface-level symptoms** but to reach into the **energetic origins of suffering**—whether they began in this lifetime, a previous one, or were passed down through your lineage.

Through experiential tools, real case reflections, and multidimensional healing methods, you will learn how to **liberate your energy**, activate your spiritual gifts, and support others through deep karmic healing sessions.

Whether you are new to Reiki or a seasoned practitioner, this book offers an invitation to go beyond the physical and into the **mystic terrain of soul memory and emotional sovereignty**.

By the end of this book, you will gain a comprehensive understanding of:

Part 1: Foundations of Karmic and Ancestral Energy

⋄ What karma truly is—and how it imprints into the soul, body, and auric field
⋄ How ancestral trauma, belief systems, and emotional patterns are passed down epigenetically and energetically
⋄ How past life memories can emerge through emotional triggers, recurring dreams, or physical symptoms
⋄ The chakra system as a map of karmic memory
⋄ The role of Reiki as a tool for awakening, clearing, and rebalancing soul-level distortions
⋄ Introduction to the Nine Spiritual Gifts, the Akashic Records, and karmic timelines

Part 2: Reiki Tools for Karmic Healing

⋄ How to use Reiki to access karmic memories and transform energetic blocks
⋄ The "I Forgives" method—a 3-step soul-clearing process for emotional and spiritual release
⋄ How to facilitate a past life regression using Reiki and intuitive techniques
⋄ Muscle testing for energetic readiness and karmic resolution
⋄ Techniques for dissolving cords and contracts (without cutting), honoring soul sovereignty
⋄ Tapping tools (BodyTalk and EFT) for sealing energetic shifts

Part 3: Releasing Contracts, Trauma, and Soul Attachments

⋄ How to identify soul contracts, loops, and attachments that are outdated
⋄ Practical tools for dissolving inherited trauma and energetic

entanglements
⋄ Full karmic healing session structure—from client intake to post-session integration
⋄ Journaling, visualization, regression scripts, and client case examples
⋄ How to hold ethical, grounded space as a karmic healing practitioner

Part 4: Reclaiming Your Soul Mission

⋄ How past life healing awakens your purpose in this lifetime
⋄ Mapping your soul mission and spiritual gifts
⋄ Aligning your health, relationships, and work with soul truth
⋄ Creating rituals for continued karmic release and spiritual embodiment
⋄ Receiving guidance from Spirit Guides, Archangels, and your Higher Self

This book is both a guide and a companion. It offers you the structure to hold sacred healing space—whether for yourself, your clients, or your lineage. You will walk away with practical Reiki-based methods, energetic understanding, and the intuitive confidence to help yourself and others release the past and live **fully in the present.**

Healing does not begin with the present moment—it begins by untangling the roots that hold it.
Reiki is the light that shows us the way.

Introduction – Healing Beyond Time with Reiki

In traditional Reiki training, we are taught to work with universal life force energy and the chakra system to support healing of the body, mind, and spirit. These foundational teachings remain vital, but there is another layer of wisdom that often lies dormant, waiting to be awakened—one that reaches beyond the physical body and even this lifetime.

As I've continued to walk the Reiki path, both as a practitioner and teacher, I've come to understand that some of our most stubborn patterns—emotional wounds, relationship struggles, physical ailments, and even self-sabotaging beliefs—aren't rooted in this life at all. They are echoes from the past. Some come from unresolved traumas passed down through our ancestral line. Others stem from karmic contracts, soul agreements, and past lives we may only sense through emotion, intuition, or dreams.

Reiki and Karmic Healing is about learning to listen to those echoes—to access and release what no longer serves the soul. Through Reiki, we are gifted a powerful tool to bring light into the unseen: to dissolve karmic patterns, reclaim lost fragments of the self, and restore harmony across the full timeline of the soul.

This book explores how to integrate Reiki with deeper spiritual techniques, including:

- Past life regression
- Ancestral energy healing
- Karmic contract release
- Akashic record access
- My signature I **Forgives** technique designed to release emotional, energetic, and karmic blocks from the root

You'll learn how to use Reiki to address patterns that feel older than this life—those moments when we say, *"Why does this keep happening to me?"* or *"I've done all the work, and it's still here."* These are often signs that the block is karmic, and Reiki gives us the tools to go deeper, not just spiritually but energetically and emotionally as well.

Throughout the chapters, you'll also discover the importance of clearing ancestral cords—not by cutting them, but by pulling them out at the root or dissolving them completely so nothing remains to regrow. You'll be introduced to new ways to muscle test for energy shifts, call upon Reiki symbols with deeper purpose, and work with your intuitive gifts to guide clients and yourself through powerful healing journeys.

Whether you are a new practitioner or a Master-level healer, this book invites you to step into your role as a soul-level guide. May it open the door to past wisdom, present power, and future peace—and remind you that healing is not linear. It's circular, spiral, and eternal.

Let us return to energy. Let us return to the soul. Let us remember who we are.

With Reiki's light and ancestral wisdom,
Dr. Constance Santego
Grand Reiki Master

PART 1:
KARMA, ENERGY, AND THE EMOTIONAL BODY

Chapter 1: What is Karma?

(Personal, Ancestral, Collective, Past Life)

Karma is more than a spiritual buzzword or the idea that "what goes around comes around." In its true essence, karma is energy in motion—created by intention, thought, word, and action. It's the vibrational residue of our choices and experiences, recorded within our soul's blueprint and carried through time. In the context of energy healing, karma represents the **unresolved energetic imprints** that influence our present state—sometimes subtly, other times profoundly.

Personal Karma

This is the energy you create in this lifetime through your actions, thoughts, and emotions. Every time you act out of fear, compassion, resentment, or love, you generate a vibrational frequency. These patterns accumulate in your auric field and can manifest as repeating life circumstances, emotional reactions, or physical symptoms. Personal karma is the most immediate and accessible to work with through Reiki.

Example: You consistently feel abandoned in relationships despite choosing different partners. This may stem from karmic energy built around self-worth or fear of intimacy created through your own current-life experiences.

Just for today, I will let go of worry and trust the flow of life.

Ancestral Karma

Also known as generational or lineage karma, ancestral karma is passed down through your family line. It can include unresolved trauma, inherited belief systems, and emotional wounds that were never fully processed. This energy is often stored in the DNA and nervous system—what science is beginning to explore through the field of **epigenetics**.

Reiki is a powerful tool for healing ancestral karma because it works non-verbally and multi-dimensionally, reaching emotional energy stored beyond conscious memory. When paired with your "I Forgives" technique, ancestral karma can be released at the root.

Example: A fear of speaking up that runs through generations of women in your family may be traced back to ancestral trauma where being visible was dangerous.

Collective Karma

This is the energetic residue shared by a group, society, culture, or humanity as a whole. War, oppression, environmental destruction, and collective belief systems create karma on a mass scale. While it may feel less personal, you are still affected by the collective energy fields you live within.

Reiki sessions that include **intention setting, visualization, and chakra clearing** can help clear the influence of collective karma—especially if you're highly empathic or sensitive to world events.

Example: Anxiety spikes when watching the news or being in crowded places may not be "yours" alone—it may be collective energy that resonates with unhealed aspects of your own journey.

Past Life Karma

This is karma created in previous lifetimes that has not yet been resolved. It often shows up as unexplained phobias, recurring dreams, strong attractions or aversions to people or places, or life patterns that seem to repeat despite inner work.

Reiki, when used with **past life regression, Akashic exploration, and the I Forgives technique**, allows you to access and dissolve these threads—without needing to fully "relive" the past.

Example: A deep fear of drowning with no logical source may be traced to a past life death at sea. Healing the energy of that experience releases the fear from your current timeline.

Reflection Prompt: "What patterns in my life feel older than this lifetime?" "Are there emotional reactions I've inherited, absorbed, or repeated?"

The Emotional Body: Where Energy Imprints Live

We are more than flesh and bone—we are energy. Surrounding and interwoven within the physical body are

Just for today, I will let go of worry and trust the flow of life.

subtle energy fields that carry our thoughts, beliefs, emotions, and spiritual experiences. One of the most important aspects of this energetic anatomy is the **emotional body**—a field of energy that holds onto every feeling we've ever experienced, whether expressed or suppressed.

It is within this layer of the aura that **karmic imprints often take root**. Emotions are not simply passing experiences— they are energetic frequencies that imprint themselves into the body's cellular memory and auric field. Over time, if not processed or cleared, these emotions can crystallize into patterns, blocks, and repeating life circumstances.

How Energy Gets Stored in the Emotional Body

When we experience intense emotions such as fear, grief, betrayal, anger, or shame, those energies don't always get fully expressed. Instead, they may get stored in the tissues, chakras, or energetic layers of the body. This is especially true for emotions we've been conditioned to suppress—or were unable to express safely at the time of the event.

These stored energies act like "programs" running in the background of our lives, influencing our perceptions, decisions, relationships, and even our physical health.

Example: A person with unprocessed grief may repeatedly manifest loss in their life—losing jobs, relationships, or even health—until that emotional frequency is acknowledged and released.

Why Karma Lives in the Emotional Body

Karma is not punishment—it's a response to energetic frequency. Because emotions carry some of the **strongest energetic charges**, they are often the "glue" that binds karmic patterns to our field.

The more emotionally charged a memory or event, the more likely it is to create a karmic imprint. And this doesn't only apply to trauma in this lifetime. Past life and ancestral experiences that carried emotional weight—fear, regret, betrayal, abandonment—can leave energetic scars that continue to influence us now.

This is why karmic healing must involve the emotional body—not just thoughts, affirmations, or spiritual insight. We must **feel to heal**.

How Reiki Heals the Emotional Body

Reiki flows where it's most needed, moving through the layers of the aura and directly into the emotional body. It softens tension, soothes stored pain, and raises the frequency of the field to gently dissolve emotional imprints.

When combined with intention, visualization, or techniques like **I Forgives**, Reiki becomes a **precision tool** for locating, lifting, and clearing stuck emotional energy—whether personal, ancestral, or karmic in origin.

Visualize: Reiki energy as a warm, intelligent light searching through your emotional body for knots, tangles, or shadows—and gently unraveling them with unconditional love.

Just for today, I will let go of worry and trust the flow of life.

Signs of a Blocked Emotional Body

- Recurring emotional triggers that feel disproportionate
- Feeling stuck or stagnant despite doing "the work"
- Unexplained sadness, heaviness, or fear
- Inability to cry or connect emotionally
- Chronic tension in the heart, solar plexus, or gut
- Repeating situations that evoke similar emotional responses

Your Emotional Energy is Sacred

Healing the emotional body is not about erasing your past. It's about **honoring it, understanding it, and releasing what no longer serves your soul's evolution.** The more you clear the emotional residue, the more space you make for joy, intuition, and freedom.

Reflection Prompts:

"What emotion do I carry the most?" "Where in my body do I feel that emotion lives?" "What might be the karmic root of that feeling?"

How the Mind Records Everything— Even Past Lives

The human mind is not limited to this lifetime. Beyond your conscious awareness lies a vast internal database—a multidimensional archive—that stores every experience your soul has ever lived. This includes not just memories from childhood, but from **ancestral experiences and past lives** as well.

We often think of the mind as the brain, but in energy medicine, the mind is a much broader system. It includes the **conscious, subconscious, unconscious, superconscious, and soul mind**—each with its own role in recording, storing, and replaying energy patterns.

These layers of mind hold the energetic signatures of:

- Past traumas and triumphs
- Emotional responses to experiences
- Belief systems inherited from ancestors
- Soul-level contracts and lessons
- Karmic "imprints" from other lifetimes

Your Mind is an Energetic Recorder

The mind acts like a camera that captures not only what happened but how it felt. It records **emotionally charged events** with greater intensity—especially when those experiences are unresolved or traumatic.

The stronger the emotion, the deeper the recording.

Just for today, I will let go of worry and trust the flow of life.

If you've ever had a flashback, an intense déjà vu moment, a dream that felt more real than reality, or an irrational fear with no logical source—this is your deeper mind trying to process what was left unfinished in your energetic history.

The subconscious mind stores these impressions in the **emotional body**, the **chakras**, and the **auric field**, which is why people can experience emotional reactions during Reiki sessions without knowing why. The energy of the memory is still present, even if the mental story has been forgotten.

Past Life Patterns Still Play Out

Even when a past life memory isn't fully remembered, its **karmic echo** can still shape your current reality. This might show up as:

- Repeating relationship dynamics (e.g., betrayal, abandonment)
- Unexplained talents or fears
- Attraction or aversion to certain places, symbols, or people
- Chronic issues that don't respond to traditional healing

These are not coincidences. They are vibrational signatures resurfacing to be acknowledged, understood, and released.

Reiki as a Tool for Unlocking the Mind

Reiki has a unique ability to bypass the analytical mind and access deeper energetic memory. When you combine Reiki with techniques such as past life regression, intuitive questioning, or your I **Forgives** method, it becomes easier to:

- Access the **root** of a repeating issue
- Dissolve emotional charge stored in the subconscious
- Rewrite the energetic script from a soul-level

You do not always need a full memory to heal the pattern. The mind simply needs **permission to release the imprint**— and Reiki provides the safe space and vibrational shift to do exactly that.

Case Insight:

A client experiences panic whenever she hears bells. Through Reiki and guided regression, she recalls a past life where bells rang before public punishment. The energy clears not by reliving the trauma but by **acknowledging the imprint**, applying Reiki to the memory, and releasing the emotional charge with "I Forgives."

Reflection Prompts:

"What recurring thought or emotional pattern feels bigger than me?" "What might my subconscious be trying to process?" "Am I open to remembering—not through words, but through energy?"

Reiki Level III (Master) and Level IV (Teacher): The Embodiment – Metal and Wood Energy

The Master level is a spiritual threshold. Here, you're not just practicing Reiki—you're becoming it.

Just for today, I will let go of worry and trust the flow of life.

Metal energy brings **refinement, precision, and integrity**, helping you discern truth from illusion. Wood brings the **vision and courage** to grow beyond your old limitations. As a Master, you become both healer and student—always evolving, always listening.

And if you choose to teach, to pass on attunements yourself, you become a **guardian of the lineage**, a living link in a chain of light stretching back to Usui and beyond. You learn not just to activate others—but to hold space for their unfolding.

An attunement is not just an energetic upgrade—it is a **sacred agreement**. One that says:
"I am ready to remember who I am."
"I am willing to be a vessel for light."
"I am open to healing—not only others, but myself."

As we explore the Five Elements in the chapters to come, remember that each Reiki level brings you closer to them—because the more you awaken your inner healer, the more aligned you become with the natural forces of the universe.

The attunement is not the destination. It's the **doorway**. And now, we walk through it—into the elemental heart of Reiki.

Understanding Energetic Conditioning

From the moment we are born—sometimes even before—our energy field begins to absorb information from our environment. This isn't just mental or emotional learning; it's **energetic conditioning**. Every word, experience, belief, and vibration we're exposed to imprints upon our energy system, shaping who we become and how we interact with the world.

Energetic conditioning is the **process by which repeated emotional, environmental, and energetic inputs form patterns** in our auric field, chakras, and nervous system. These patterns eventually crystallize into habits, identities, beliefs, and behaviors—some helpful, some limiting, and many unconscious.

Where Does Energetic Conditioning Come From?

1. **Family Systems & Ancestral Beliefs**
   - We inherit energetic patterns just as we inherit eye color or facial features.
   - If your family line carried unhealed trauma, scarcity mindsets, shame, or emotional repression, those frequencies can become the baseline of your energy field—until you intentionally shift them.
2. **Cultural & Societal Norms**
   - The collective beliefs of your culture or society (e.g., what success looks like, what roles men/women "should" play, how emotions are treated) also condition your energy.

Just for today, I will let go of worry and trust the flow of life.

- o These often become subconscious rules that restrict spiritual growth.

3. **Early Childhood Experiences**
   - o Our foundational energy is shaped most deeply in childhood, when our aura is still highly open and sensitive.
   - o Repeated messages—spoken or unspoken— about love, worth, safety, or power imprint deeply, even before language develops.

4. **Reinforced Emotional Loops**
   - o Emotional patterns are "reinforced" over time through repetition.
   - o For example, the more often a person feels unworthy, the more that vibration embeds itself in their field, attracting more experiences that confirm it—until it's cleared.

Conditioning Isn't Always Logical—It's Energetic

One of the challenges with energetic conditioning is that it doesn't respond to logic or affirmations alone. You may know intellectually that you are safe, lovable, or capable— but your energy system may still be running old programs that say otherwise.

This is why healing at the energetic level is so important. Reiki helps **gently deactivate the old programming** by introducing a new frequency—one of balance, harmony, and unconditional love.

Breaking Conditioning with Reiki + Intention

When you combine Reiki with awareness, intention, and forgiveness techniques, you begin to **recondition the energy field**.

You can:

- Use Reiki to target the chakras or areas of the body where that conditioning is stored
- Visualize clearing or rewriting old programs
- Speak or silently intend new beliefs while channeling energy
- Use muscle testing to identify what pattern is running and whether it has been cleared
- Apply *I Forgives* to emotional components of the conditioning

Example: "I forgive myself for believing I'm not good enough." → Apply Reiki to the solar plexus while repeating this until the emotional charge softens.

Energetic Conditioning Can Be Karmic

Sometimes, the conditioning isn't from this lifetime at all. It may have been shaped by:

- A vow made in a past life (e.g., "I will never speak again")
- A traumatic death that created fear of visibility or power
- A karmic lesson carried across incarnations

Just for today, I will let go of worry and trust the flow of life.

These are the moments when energy healing must go deeper than the present—into the timelines of the soul.

Reflection Prompts:

"What beliefs do I carry that aren't truly mine?" "Where did I learn them—from whom or what?" "What part of me is ready to release that conditioning and return to truth?"

Featured Concept: "We Live by Emotions, Not Thoughts"

We often like to believe that logic rules our lives—that our decisions are made by reason and that our thoughts shape our reality. But in truth, it is **our emotions that drive us**. Emotions are the fuel behind our actions, reactions, and energetic imprinting. Thoughts may offer direction, but it is our feelings that move us.

This is why energetic healing—especially karmic and ancestral healing—must begin with **emotional awareness and release**. The emotional body is where karma embeds, where trauma is stored, and where transformation begins.

Why Emotions Are More Powerful Than Thoughts

1. **Emotions Activate the Energy Field**
   - Emotions carry a frequency. That frequency determines how we vibrate and what we attract.
   - Love, fear, shame, joy, guilt, peace—each has a distinct resonance in the aura and chakras.
2. **Emotions Drive Behavior**
   - You may think you've made a logical decision, but it's often based on a desire to feel safe, validated, loved, or in control.
   - This is why the same thoughts can lead to different outcomes depending on your emotional state.
3. **The Subconscious Responds to Emotion**

Just for today, I will let go of worry and trust the flow of life.

- o The subconscious mind—where karmic memory lives—is **emotionally driven**, not rational.
- o When emotional energy is stored from past experiences (especially traumatic ones), it creates a repeating vibrational signal until cleared.

4. **We Remember What We Feel**
   - o Past life and early childhood memories are often accessed first through **emotion**, not logic or language.
   - o You may not remember the details, but the *feeling* remains—and shapes your reactions.

Why This Matters in Karmic Healing

If your healing work only addresses thoughts (like affirmations or mindset work), you may see temporary relief—but the deeper issue will persist if the emotional charge remains in your field.

To dissolve karmic patterns:

- You must **access the emotional memory**—even if you don't recall the original event.
- You must **acknowledge, allow, and release** that emotion at the energetic level.
- Tools like **Reiki, "I Forgives", regression,** and **tapping** work because they interact with emotional energy, not just thoughts.

What This Might Look Like in a Session

A client says, "I know I'm worthy. I've done all the affirmations."
But when you place your hands over their heart chakra, you feel grief.
Reiki reveals the truth: The body still holds pain that the mind is trying to override.
Through "I Forgives," breath, and energy, the grief begins to move.
Only then can worthiness fully integrate—not just as a thought but as a lived emotion.

Reflection Prompts:

"What emotion is behind the story I keep telling myself?"
"What do I feel most often when I'm triggered?"
"Where in my life am I thinking one thing but feeling another?"

Just for today, I will let go of worry and trust the flow of life.

Soul Reflection: Susannah in the Void

*(from Journey of a Soul)**
Soft Cover ISBN: 978-1-7772220-7-9

In *Journey of a Soul*, Susannah finds herself trapped in the Void after death—not because she was evil or wrong, but because she lacked **belief in anything beyond the material world**. Her soul, heavy with doubt and spiritual disconnection, could not cross into the Light. She wandered in confusion, unable to ascend, until Lexi, the story's guide and healer, reached her through compassion, spiritual clarity, and energetic truth.

Susannah's story is more than a fictional account—it is an archetype of **spiritual amnesia** and the emotional weight of **unresolved karmic energy**.

The Void as a Symbol of Unhealed Karma

The Void in Susannah's journey represents the energetic state many people unknowingly live in:

- Emotionally numb but intellectually active
- Spiritually blocked despite physical health
- Repeating patterns without understanding why

It is a place of **disconnection from Source**, caused not only by choices in this lifetime but also by **ancestral disconnection, inherited belief systems, and soul trauma from other lifetimes**.

Susannah's Karma Was Emotional, Not Moral

Karma isn't always about what we did wrong—it's about **what is left unresolved**.

In Susannah's case, it was her **denial of the spiritual world**, her resistance to trust, and her emotionally suppressed grief that created the karmic condition. She wasn't being punished. She was simply magnetized to the frequency she carried: confusion, fear, and disbelief.

Her journey mirrors many real-life experiences:

- People who keep seeking, but feel stuck
- Clients who say, "I've tried everything," but haven't touched the emotional root
- Healers who feel empty, despite their knowledge, because their soul is still carrying unseen weight

How This Reflects in Karmic Healing Work

In karmic healing, we often meet "Susannahs"—souls who are seeking peace but haven't yet found it because:

- Their emotional body is blocked with suppressed grief or shame
- They inherited disbelief in healing or spirituality
- Their soul remembers a trauma from another lifetime that was never processed

Reiki helps lift the veil. It reaches into the energetic memory and gently brings the soul back into resonance with the Light.

Just for today, I will let go of worry and trust the flow of life.

But like Lexi, we must meet each soul—our own or a client's—with compassion, not judgment.

You cannot force someone into the Light. But you can hold the frequency until they remember it's real.

Reflection Prompts:

"Where in my life have I doubted what I couldn't see?"
"What emotional energy might be keeping part of me stuck in the Void?"
"Am I ready to invite that part of me back into the Light?"

PART 2.
PAST LIFE REGRESSION
WITH REIKI

Just for today, I will let go of worry and trust the flow of life.

Chapter 2: Past Life Regression with Reiki

Why Past Life Work Matters in Healing Today

Past life healing isn't just about spiritual curiosity—it's about breaking free from invisible patterns that no longer serve the soul in this lifetime. Whether or not you remember your past lives consciously, the **energy of those experiences still lives in your field**, shaping your emotions, relationships, beliefs, and even physical health.

At the soul level, nothing is lost. Every lesson, vow, trauma, and triumph leaves an imprint. These imprints—especially the unresolved ones—can ripple into the present through karmic loops, emotional triggers, soul contracts, and unconscious behaviors.

When you begin to work with past life energy through Reiki, you're not simply looking backward. You're **activating healing across timelines**, allowing your current life to evolve more freely, more consciously, and more joyfully.

Signs You May Be Carrying Past Life Energy

- Irrational fears or phobias with no known cause
- Recurring relationship dynamics (e.g., betrayal, abandonment, power struggles)

- Strong, unexplainable attraction or repulsion to places, cultures, people, or symbols
- Chronic physical symptoms with no medical explanation
- Deep-rooted guilt, grief, shame, or fear that feels disproportionate
- Dreams that feel more like memories than imagination
- A sense of "I've been here before" or déjà vu in spiritual settings

Example: A person who cannot speak in front of groups despite years of training may be carrying a past life wound related to persecution or public punishment.

Why Reiki is the Ideal Tool for Past Life Healing

Reiki opens the energetic pathways between your present life and soul memory. Unlike hypnosis, which requires mental focus, Reiki flows through **intuitive, emotional, and spiritual channels**, allowing the subconscious to reveal what the conscious mind may block.

Because Reiki works beyond the limits of time and space, it's especially effective for:

- Soothing the emotional charge of traumatic past-life experiences
- Restoring lost soul fragments
- Healing wounds across lifetimes without the need to "relive" the pain
- Creating safe energetic space for integration

Just for today, I will let go of worry and trust the flow of life.

When paired with intention, visualization, and techniques like **guided regression or "I Forgives,"** Reiki becomes a sacred bridge between the soul's history and its evolution.

Past Life Work Isn't About Fixation—It's About Freedom

The purpose of exploring past lives is not to escape the present or dramatize the past. It's to bring light to the hidden energy affecting your current experience.

Once acknowledged and energetically released, karmic imprints no longer need to express themselves through suffering. You gain access to **new choices**, deeper self-understanding, and spiritual sovereignty.

You're not doomed to repeat what you remember. You're empowered to heal what you carry.

Reflection Prompts:

"What issue in my life feels older than me?"
"What do I feel drawn to… or afraid of… for no apparent reason?"
"Am I open to what my soul wants to show me—even if I don't understand it right away?"

Signs You're Living a Past Life Pattern

Most people are unaware they're being influenced by past life energy—yet the signs are often hiding in plain sight. These patterns can feel like a **"loop"** you're stuck in, repeating with different people, circumstances, or settings, but always with the same emotional or energetic outcome.

These are not coincidences. They're clues.

When a soul lesson remains incomplete or when a karmic contract hasn't yet been released, that energy seeks expression in the present—often through your **relationships, fears, emotions, or even your body.**

Common Signs You're Replaying a Past Life Pattern

1. **Recurring Life Situations or Themes**
   You've changed jobs, partners, or locations… yet the *same* dynamic keeps playing out.

   Example: You keep attracting controlling partners or feeling powerless, even when you've done the inner work.

2. **Unexplained Emotional Reactions**
   Overwhelming fear, grief, rage, or anxiety in situations that don't justify it.

   Example: Panic before crossing bridges, fear of water, or extreme sadness when hearing a specific name.

Just for today, I will let go of worry and trust the flow of life.

3. **Instant Soul Connections (Positive or Negative)**
   Feeling deeply connected—or intensely repelled—by someone upon first meeting them.

   These are often karmic relationships: lovers, rivals, allies, or mentors returning to resolve unfinished business.

4. **Repetitive Dreams or "Memory-Like" Visions**
   Vivid dreamscapes that feel more like memories than fantasy.

   You may "see" yourself in a different time, culture, or body—repeating key events or moments.

5. **Unexplainable Talents or Fears**
   Natural skills (like languages, music, or healing abilities) or phobias that emerge without training or trauma in this life.

   Example: A child who plays piano masterfully without lessons or someone with a fear of swords, fire, or imprisonment.

6. **Karmic Relationships with a Heavy Emotional Pull**
   Deep connections that feel fated, magnetic, or emotionally charged—are often marked by difficulty, obsession, or rapid growth.

   These relationships often come with spiritual contracts to fulfill or complete.

7. **Chronic Physical Ailments Without Clear Cause**
   Especially when centered around the throat, heart, gut, or spine—these may correlate to wounds or deaths from other lives.

Why These Signs Matter

Your soul is trying to **complete a story**, not punish you.

These signs are not curses or punishments—they are opportunities to release, rewrite, and realign your energy. The repetition is the soul's way of saying:

"Let's finish this now… so we can move forward."

When you recognize a pattern as karmic, you can:

- Stop blaming yourself or others
- Detach from shame, guilt, or resentment
- Use Reiki to soothe and clear the imprint
- Apply the **I Forgives** technique to complete the lesson emotionally
- Invite soul-level healing and transformation

Reflection Prompts:

"What situation in my life feels like a broken record?"
"Is there someone I feel deeply tied to, even though our relationship is difficult?"
"What emotional response do I carry that feels older than this lifetime?"

Just for today, I will let go of worry and trust the flow of life.

How to Use Reiki to Initiate a Regression Session

Reiki is not only a healing tool—it's a spiritual gateway. Because Reiki flows beyond the limits of time and space, it's an ideal vehicle for accessing soul memory, including past life experiences. When combined with intention, breathwork, visualization, and grounding techniques, Reiki can gently guide the practitioner or client into a **regression state**—a relaxed, intuitive awareness where past-life impressions can rise to the surface.

This approach does not rely on hypnosis or external prompting—it works by opening energetic channels, calming the nervous system, and allowing the subconscious mind to reveal what the soul is ready to process.

Pre-Session Preparation

Before beginning a regression session, it's important to:

- **Set a clear intention:**
  "I am ready to be shown the past life (or lives) most affecting my current issue."
- **Create a safe, grounded space:**
  Use Reiki to clear the room, call in protection, and establish energetic boundaries.
- **Activate your Reiki flow:**
  Place your hands over your heart or crown and mentally or verbally invite Reiki to flow for the highest good of the session.

- **Center and ground:**
  Spend a few minutes in meditation or breathwork, focusing on the soles of the feet or the root chakra to remain grounded throughout the experience.

The Regression Process with Reiki

You can guide yourself or a client through a past life regression by following this simple, intuitive structure. Modify as needed based on your practice.

Step 1: Reiki Activation and Relaxation

- Begin by placing your hands on your third eye or heart center.
- Send Reiki into your entire auric field.
- Visualize a soft golden or violet light surrounding you.
- Invite the subconscious to relax and the higher self to guide.

Step 2: Enter the Soul Memory Space

Use this visualization or script:

"Imagine a train station in front of you. This station leads to your soul's memories. A train pulls in. You step aboard. You find a seat and close your eyes. When you next open them, you'll be in the lifetime that holds a lesson, pattern, or insight relevant to your current healing."

Just for today, I will let go of worry and trust the flow of life.

Use Reiki hand placements (one hand on the solar plexus, one on the heart) to keep the emotional body calm and open during this process.

Step 3: Observation and Sensory Exploration

Once the scene or impression arises, explore it without judgment. Ask yourself or your client:

- What are you wearing?
- Are you indoors or outdoors?
- Do you sense your age, gender, or role?
- What emotion are you feeling?
- Who is around you? Do you recognize anyone?

Stay open to symbols, sensations, or fragments. Reiki will help guide what's relevant to rise to the surface.

Step 4: Identify the Karmic Thread

Ask:

"What lesson was learned (or not learned) in that life?" "How is this connected to what I'm experiencing now?"

As the answers arise—through words, emotion, images, or intuition—allow Reiki to flow through your hands to integrate and calm.

Step 5: Clear the Emotional Charge

Now that you've identified the emotional imprint, use Reiki to begin clearing:

- Place your hands over the corresponding chakra (e.g., heart for grief, solar plexus for fear).
- Breathe deeply.
- Use the "I Forgives" method:
  - Forgive yourself in that life
  - Forgive others involved
  - Allow them to forgive you

You may also invite any remaining energy to **dissolve, be returned to the Source, or transmuted** into peace and wisdom.

Step 6: Integration and Closure

- Visualize the past-life version of yourself stepping into the light or merging with your current self.
- Thank the soul for showing you the memory.
- Visualize golden light sealing and blessing your aura.
- Ground deeply (touch your feet, drink water, or place hands on your thighs).
- End with a brief reflection or journaling to capture insights.

Important Tips

- Don't chase the memory—let it come naturally.
- Emotional responses (crying, sighing, body tension) are signs that energy is moving.
- You may not get a full story—and that's okay. **Emotion and energy** are what need healing.
- Always anchor the client or yourself before closing the session.

Just for today, I will let go of worry and trust the flow of life.

Reflection Prompts:

"What did I feel, and where in my body did I feel it?"
"What emotional thread connected that life to my current one?"
"What am I ready to release or reclaim?"

Step-by-Step Technique: The Train Ride Regression

One of the simplest and most effective ways to access past life memory is through the **"Train Ride Regression"**—a guided visualization that uses the metaphor of a train to gently transport the mind into a soul memory space.

This technique allows the subconscious to present past-life experiences in a safe, symbolic, and emotionally manageable way. Combined with Reiki energy and emotional clearing tools like *I Forgives*, this method becomes a powerful entry point for karmic healing.

Before You Begin, Prepare the Space

Whether you are guiding someone else or doing the journey yourself:

- Activate Reiki energy
- Ground your energy with breath or root chakra visualization
- State a clear intention:

  "I am ready to remember a past life that is currently affecting me and is ready to be healed."

- Create an energetically safe and sacred space
- Keep a journal, tissues, and water nearby

Just for today, I will let go of worry and trust the flow of life.

Train Ride Regression: A Guided Journey

Use this step-by-step guide as a spoken script, recorded meditation, or silent inner visualization:

Step 1: Relax and Receive Reiki

Close your eyes. Feel the flow of Reiki washing over you like warm sunlight. Breathe deeply into your belly. With each breath, let tension melt away. Let Reiki fill your aura with light and peace.

Step 2: Arrive at the Train Station

"Imagine yourself standing at a beautiful old train station. It's peaceful here. A light mist floats through the air, and a sense of timelessness surrounds you."

"This is not an ordinary train station—it is the gateway to your soul's memories. As you look around, you notice a train pulling in. It's your train. It knows exactly where to take you."

Step 3: Board the Soul Train

"You step aboard. The train is warm and welcoming. As you settle into a seat, you feel Reiki energy flowing through the cabin like a soft breeze, keeping you safe and grounded."

"You hear the conductor's voice gently say: 'We're going to the lifetime that is most important for your healing today.'"

"As the train begins to move, you feel yourself going deeper—past time, past space, into the soul's memory."

Step 4: Arrival in a Past Life

"The train comes to a smooth stop. The door opens. You step out onto solid ground."

"As you look around, what do you see? Is it day or night? Are you inside or outside? What's the temperature?"

"Look down at your feet—what are you wearing? Are you male or female? Young or old?"

"Where are you? What's happening around you? Who is with you?"

"Breathe and allow Reiki to hold you as images, emotions, or sensations come forward. There is no right or wrong—only experience."

Step 5: Explore the Life

"Allow yourself to witness an important moment in this life. You may see it, feel it, or simply know it."

"What lesson or emotion is present here? What unfinished energy wants your attention?"

Keep your hands over your heart or solar plexus if you are guiding Reiki during this part.

Step 6: Move to the Moment of Transition

"Now you are at the end of this past life. You are safe, and you are witnessing your soul leaving the body."

Just for today, I will let go of worry and trust the flow of life.

"What emotion or energy are you carrying with you as you leave this life? Is there a message? A regret? A soul vow?"

Reiki can now flow deeply to help clear or integrate this moment.

Step 7: Heal and Release

"From this place of soul wisdom, you may now choose to release any energy that no longer serves you."

"Use the *I Forgives* technique: Forgive yourself, forgive others, and allow them to forgive you."

"Invite Reiki to transmute any leftover energy into pure light."

"When you're ready, thank this life and return to the train."

Step 8: Return to the Present

"The train gently carries you back through time. You return to the station, bringing with you any wisdom, peace, or release you've gained."

"Breathe deeply. Wiggle your fingers and toes. Ground yourself by placing your hands on your legs or feet."

"When you're ready, open your eyes."

After the Journey

- **Journal your experience**: even fragments matter—emotions, symbols, scenery.
- **Hydrate and rest**: regression work can be energetically deepening.
- **Use Reiki or grounding practices** to fully integrate.

Reflection Prompts:

"What was the central emotion in that lifetime?"
"What patterns or themes echoed into my current life?"
"What wisdom or energy am I now reclaiming?"

Just for today, I will let go of worry and trust the flow of life.

How to Interpret Symbols, Emotions, and Stories in Past Life Regression

Past life regression is not always a movie-like memory that plays out in vivid detail. More often, it unfolds through symbols, emotional waves, intuitive impressions, or short story-like fragments. This can leave some people wondering if they "made it up" or if it really happened.

But in energetic and soul-based healing, it's **not about the literal accuracy of what you saw—it's about the emotional truth and energetic imprint it carries**.

The language of the soul is **symbolic, emotional, and nonlinear**. Learning to interpret this language is key to unlocking wisdom. The language of the soul is **symbolic, emotional, and nonlinear**. Learning to interpret this language is key to unlocking the wisdom and clearing the energetic residue that past life experiences leave behind.

Just like dreams, past life regressions speak in metaphors and sensations. Your conscious mind may want a clear storyline, names, and dates—but your **subconscious only reveals what your soul is ready to process**, and it often does so through symbolic representation.

Trust What You Feel Over What You See

You might expect a vivid, full-color movie to play out—but instead, you get a brief flash, a wave of sadness, or the image of a door that won't open. That's not a failure. That *is* the regression.

The energy you feel is more important than the scene you witness.

Ask:

- What emotion arose with that image?
- What part of my body responded?
- Does that feeling exist in my life now?

Common Past Life Symbols and What They May Represent

Symbol	Possible Meaning
Locked doors	Blocked memory, suppressed trauma
Floods or drowning	Overwhelm, fear of emotion, death by water
Fire or burning	Transformation, purification, or persecution trauma
Repeated numbers	Timelines, contracts, patterns
Chains or cages	Oppression, soul vows, karmic entrapment
Keys or scrolls	Knowledge or wisdom being reclaimed
Mirrors	Identity, self-reflection, soul recognition

Just for today, I will let go of worry and trust the flow of life.

Symbol	Possible Meaning
Falling or flying	Soul transitions, release, ascension, death
Animals (e.g., snakes, horses, wolves)	Guides, fear totem, past life companions

These are just frameworks—*your personal meaning* is always the most accurate. Reiki helps deepen your intuitive clarity during and after regression to feel what the symbols mean for **you**.

Emotional Overlays Are Clues to the Lesson

Past life healing is never about perfection—it's about **resolution**. And that resolution always starts with emotion.

If you felt guilt in the regression, the karma is likely about self-forgiveness.
If you felt anger, the pattern may involve injustice, betrayal, or power imbalance.
If you felt longing, there may be a soul contract or loss still influencing your path.

Use Reiki to move energy through the chakras and emotional body—especially in the **heart, solar plexus**, and **sacral centers**, where most karmic residue is stored.

When the Mind Doubts the Memory

It's normal to wonder:

"Did I make that up?"

That question often arises when the **ego mind tries to protect you** from something uncomfortable, unfamiliar, or deeply spiritual. The truth is, your soul doesn't care whether it's "historically accurate"—it's offering what you need to heal now.

Use this mantra after a session:

"What I experienced is real enough to be healed."

Reflection Prompts:

"What did I feel during the regression?"
"What did that symbol mean to me?"
"What old story or wound might this experience be trying to resolve?"
"Am I ready to let go of what I no longer need to carry—across time?"

Just for today, I will let go of worry and trust the flow of life.

Creating a Regression Journal

A **Regression Journal** is a sacred tool for tracking, integrating, and understanding the past life experiences that surface during your healing journey. Whether you're doing self-guided regressions or working with a practitioner, journaling allows you to capture the emotional and symbolic threads before they fade and reflect on recurring patterns over time.

The journal becomes your **soul map**—a place to gather insights, release old energy, and document your healing journey across lifetimes.

Why Journal After Regression?

- The subconscious mind processes in fragments—journaling helps **piece the story together**.
- Writing anchors the experience into your conscious awareness, helping you make sense of emotions and symbols.
- Your intuitive mind will often **reveal more while you write**—unexpected connections may emerge.
- Journals help track patterns that reappear in multiple sessions or dreams.

What to Include After Each Regression Session

Create dedicated pages or templates with space to record:

Session Details:

- Date / Time

- Intention or focus of the session
- Method used (e.g., Train Ride Regression, Reiki with visualization, guided audio)

Impressions Received:

- Images, symbols, or scenes
- Emotions felt (before, during, after)
- Physical sensations or energy shifts
- Sounds, names, smells, places
- Any standout characters or figures

Energetic Themes:

- Role you played in the lifetime (e.g., caregiver, warrior, mystic)
- Main lesson, wound, or unresolved energy
- Repeating patterns that mirror this lifetime

Integration Notes:

- Reiki hand placements or chakras activated
- Use of "I Forgives" statements
- Muscle testing results (if used)
- Post-session mood, physical effects, dreams

Takeaway Message:

- What wisdom did your soul offer you?
- What energy did you release or reclaim?
- What do you choose to do differently now?

Just for today, I will let go of worry and trust the flow of life.

Example Entry Snapshot:

Date: April 8, 2025
Focus: Anxiety around public speaking
Past Life Scene: Male scribe in ancient Rome, executed for sharing spiritual scrolls
Emotion: Panic, shame, silencing
Symbol: Broken ink quill = voice suppression
Healing: Heart + throat chakra Reiki, forgiveness of persecutors
Message: "Your voice is safe now."
Shift: Booked a podcast interview the next day with calmness

Optional Enhancements:

- Color-coding entries based on emotion or chakra
- Drawing symbols or scenes from the vision
- Adding "moon phase" or "astrological season" at time of session
- Creating a "soul wisdom" page at the back for quotes, messages, or synchronicities

Reflection Prompts:

"What energy am I carrying forward from that life?"
"Is this a pattern I've seen before?"
"What part of me is finally ready to be free?"

Tool: Regression Template

One of the most powerful ways to deepen and integrate your past life healing work is by keeping a **regression journal**. After each session—whether self-guided or facilitated—capturing your impressions, emotions, and insights helps you make sense of the experience, track patterns, and notice healing progress over time.

This Printable Regression Template is designed to be **simple, intuitive, and emotionally focused**, in alignment with your Reiki-based karmic healing approach. It can be used by individuals or practitioners guiding others.

How to Use This Template

After completing a regression (via the Train Ride technique, Reiki journeying, or other guided methods), take a few moments to ground yourself. Then sit quietly with this form and fill it out intuitively—*what matters is what you felt, not how much you remember.*

Tip: Have a printed stack available for client sessions or your own soul journaling practice. It's also a beautiful addition to your course workbook or healing journal.

Just for today, I will let go of worry and trust the flow of life.

Past Life Regression Record Template

1. Date & Time of Session:

_____

2. Who Led the Session?

☐ Self-guided   ☐ Practitioner-guided
Practitioner Name (if applicable):

_____

3. Initial Intention / Focus of the Session:

(What were you seeking insight or healing for?)

_____

_____

4. Setting or Scene Observed:

(Describe any landscape, location, structures, or period you noticed.)

_____

_____

5. Role or Identity in That Life:

(Any sense of your age, gender, culture, personality, or role?)

_____

_____

6. People or Beings You Encountered:

(Who appeared? Did anyone feel familiar? Soul connections?)

_____

_____

7. Emotions Experienced in That Life:

☐ Fear ☐ Grief ☐ Love ☐ Anger ☐ Guilt
☐ Shame
☐ Hope ☐ Loss ☐ Confusion ☐ Joy ☐
Longing
Other:

_____

8. Symbols or Images That Stood Out:

(Describe any metaphors, animals, objects, colors, or recurring signs.)

_____

_____

9. Message or Lesson From the Life:

(What insight or soul wisdom came through?)

_____

_____

Just for today, I will let go of worry and trust the flow of life.

10. What Needs to Be Healed or Released?

☐ Emotional Pattern   ☐ Karmic Contract   ☐
Ancestral Energy
☐ Soul Vow   ☐ Physical Imprint   ☐ Relationship
Dynamic
Details:

_____

11. How Did Reiki Support the Session?

☐ Helped me stay calm
☐ Amplified intuitive impressions
☐ Brought emotional release
☐ Created a safe space
☐ Supported forgiveness or closure
Notes:

_____

12. Did You Use "I Forgives"?

☐ Yes   ☐ No   If yes, what was forgiven or released?

_____

13. Final Thoughts, Feelings, or Aftercare Needed:

_____

_____

_____

Client Example:

When a Fear of Water Was Healed After Visiting a Drowning Life

Some karmic patterns hide in plain sight—masquerading as phobias, habits, or unexplainable fears. One of the most common signs of past life trauma is a persistent emotional reaction that has **no logical origin** in the current lifetime.

This was the case with *Maya* (name changed), a client who came to me with an intense, lifelong fear of water. She couldn't swim, avoided lakes and pools, and even experienced anxiety while showering if water touched her face unexpectedly. No childhood trauma or near-drowning event could explain her response.

The Regression Journey

We began with grounding, intention setting, and a gentle *Train Ride Regression* while channeling Reiki into her heart and solar plexus.

As the session unfolded, tears began streaming down Maya's face. She described an image that came to her mind—not like a dream, but like a flash of memory:

"I'm a young woman... and I'm trapped... in a sinking ship. It's dark. Cold. People are screaming. I can't get out. I die underwater."

Just for today, I will let go of worry and trust the flow of life.

She gasped at the vividness of it. Her body even began to shiver slightly as the emotional imprint surfaced.

The Emotional Pattern Revealed

The fear she had always felt around water wasn't about the water itself. It was about the *emotion* associated with that memory—**helplessness, terror, and unfinished death energy**.

The trauma hadn't been released after the lifetime ended. It had followed her soul into this incarnation, embedding itself into her **emotional body and cellular memory**. Even though her current self had never been in danger, her *soul remembered*.

Reiki + I Forgives in Action

While gently channeling Reiki to the heart and throat chakras, I guided Maya through the *I Forgives* process:

- "I forgive myself for not surviving."
- "I forgive the crew for abandoning us."
- "I allow myself to forgive the sea and what I believed it took from me."
- "I allow my soul to forgive me for carrying this pain into this life."

As she spoke, her breathing softened. She placed her hands over her chest and smiled through the tears.

"It feels like something heavy just left me."

After the Session

In the weeks that followed, Maya began slowly testing her comfort around water. She visited a lake with her partner and dipped her feet in—no panic. Then, weeks later, she booked her first swimming lesson. The fear was gone.

She hadn't simply "gotten over it." She had healed the **root**— emotionally, energetically, and karmically.

Why This Matters

This story is a reminder that:

- *Phobias and intense fears often stem from unresolved past life trauma.*
- Reiki can safely bring those memories to the surface and help dissolve their emotional charge.
- You don't have to understand everything consciously to experience soul-level healing.
- Healing is not about erasing the past, but about **integrating its wisdom and releasing its weight.**

Just for today, I will let go of worry and trust the flow of life.

Cross-Link Resource: Past Life Regression with Reiki

Video Title: Guided Past Life Regression for Emotional Healing
Watch it here: https://youtu.be/TWHBfZeToOU

This companion video gently guides you through a **Reiki-supported past life regression journey**, helping you access memories, emotions, or energetic patterns that may still influence your present-day life.

Whether you're working through karmic themes, relationship wounds, or spiritual blocks, this video offers a safe and supportive container for exploration and release.

In This Video, You'll Experience:

- A calming induction into the subconscious memory field
- A step-by-step guided journey to one of your past lives
- Reiki-infused energy to support safety, clarity, and emotional integration
- Gentle prompts to uncover the soul lessons from that life

Suggested Uses:

- As part of your *Past Life Regression with Reiki* chapter
- Before or after completing the "Train Ride Regression" technique
- Anytime you feel the presence of an old pattern or energy that isn't "you"
- To gently reconnect with your soul's wisdom and release hidden karmic residue

Your soul remembers. This video helps you listen, feel, and release—so you can move forward with lightness and clarity.

Just for today, I will let go of worry and trust the flow of life.

PART 3:

HEALING THE

ANCESTRAL LINEAGE

Chapter 3: Healing the Ancestral Lineage

Healing the Ancestral Lineage

Epigenetics and Energetic DNA

We are not just a product of our own choices—we are the living expression of generations before us. Every person carries a **spiritual and biological inheritance** passed down through their lineage, including memories, traumas, coping mechanisms, beliefs, and energetic patterns. These inherited imprints live in both our DNA and our energy field.

Modern science is beginning to confirm what healers and mystics have long known: the past lives on in us—not just symbolically, but **biologically and energetically**.

What is Epigenetics?

Epigenetics is the study of how **environmental influences, trauma, stress, and behavior can change the expression of genes**—without altering the DNA sequence itself. These changes can be passed down through generations.

In simple terms, **trauma can be inherited**, and so can resilience.

Just for today, I will let go of worry and trust the flow of life.

Scientific studies (such as those involving the descendants of Holocaust survivors or families affected by famine) have shown that emotional and physical trauma leaves a chemical "mark" on genes—affecting stress response, hormone production, immunity, and mental health for future generations.

What is Energetic DNA?

Beyond our physical DNA lies our **energetic DNA**—the vibrational record of our ancestral line, including:

- Unprocessed grief or guilt
- Patterns of addiction, shame, or abuse
- Religious, cultural, or spiritual vows
- Familial beliefs about success, safety, love, or power
- Gifts, strengths, and sacred knowledge passed down energetically

These energetic imprints are stored in the **root chakra, the base of the spine**, and the **epigenetic field around the auric body**, often revealed in Reiki sessions as heaviness, pulsing, or blockages in the lower chakras.

Inherited vs. Self-Created Karma

Some energy you're carrying was created in this life. But often, what you're healing is **not just yours**. It's part of your **ancestral burden**.

"This pain didn't start with me, but it can end with me."

By recognizing this, we release guilt and embrace the sacred opportunity to be the **breaker of cycles**—the one who transforms pain into peace for generations past and future.

Reiki's Role in Ancestral Healing

Reiki flows through time. It can access the energetic DNA encoded in your lineage and:

- Soothe emotional trauma held by ancestors
- Release inherited belief systems (e.g., "we don't speak our truth" or "we always suffer in love")
- Dissolve energetic cords passed through generations
- Restore strengths and soul gifts buried by family history
- Bring peace to those who came before you—and through that, to you

Reiki symbols, especially when combined with intention and visualization, can **unravel ancestral energy blockages** from the root. Your *I Forgives* method is especially effective here when directed toward family lines.

Signs of Ancestral Karma or Energetic Inheritance

- You feel burdened by family responsibility, guilt, or obligation
- You've repeated the same patterns as parents or grandparents
- Certain illnesses or emotional struggles run in the family
- You feel disconnected from your roots or cultural identity

Just for today, I will let go of worry and trust the flow of life.

- You've had vivid dreams or visions of ancestors calling out
- There's tension in your body when discussing or remembering family events

Reflection Prompts:

"What emotional or life pattern feels older than me?"
"Do I carry beliefs or fears that match my parents or grandparents?"
"Am I ready to heal this for myself—and for them?"

How Trauma is Passed Through Generations

When we think of trauma, we often picture a personal, isolated experience—something that happened to us. But trauma doesn't always begin with us. In truth, we often carry the emotional and energetic residue of events that occurred **generations ago**. These inherited wounds can shape our behavior, beliefs, health, and relationships, even when we have no conscious awareness of the original source.

This is known as **generational trauma**—and it is one of the most profound forms of karma we can heal with Reiki.

Generational Trauma: What It Is and How It Spreads

Trauma is not only emotional—it's energetic. When a traumatic event is not processed, the energy of it remains in the person's system and can be:

- **Encoded in the DNA** through epigenetic markers
- **Imprinted into the emotional body** and auric field
- **Stored in the nervous system** and passed through stress responses
- **Energetically transferred** through unconscious behavior, belief, or suppressed memory

This trauma is then unconsciously passed down through:

- Stories (or silence)
- Family dynamics
- Unspoken fears

Just for today, I will let go of worry and trust the flow of life.

- Survival patterns and coping mechanisms

Science Confirms the Legacy of Trauma

Studies have shown that descendants of people who experienced war, genocide, slavery, abuse, or famine often carry altered stress responses and hormone levels—even if they've never personally experienced those events.

These inherited changes affect:

- Emotional regulation
- Fear and anxiety levels
- Resilience or vulnerability to depression
- Relationship dynamics
- Identity and self-worth

Signs You May Be Carrying Generational Trauma

- You experience intense emotional reactions you can't explain
- You carry shame, fear, or guilt that doesn't seem to belong to you
- There's a repeating pattern in your family line (abuse, addiction, abandonment, silence)
- You feel responsible for your family's emotional well-being
- You struggle to set boundaries with relatives
- You feel disconnected from your ancestry, culture, or spiritual roots
- You've done a lot of personal healing—but something still "won't release."

Reiki's Role in Generational Trauma Healing

Reiki is gentle, non-invasive, and deeply spiritual—making it ideal for ancestral and generational healing. It does not require you to *know* the exact story to begin healing it. Energy goes where it is needed most.

With Reiki, you can:

- Direct energy to the **root chakra** (ancestral foundation)
- Visualize healing flowing **backward through your family line**
- Use the *I Forgives* method to release blame, shame, and silence
- Channel peace and closure to ancestors who couldn't complete their healing
- Invite forward ancestral gifts, not just pain

"I heal what they could not. I honor them by becoming free."

A Simple Ancestral Reiki Practice

1. Place your hands on your lower abdomen (root area).
2. Call upon your lineage—seen and unseen.
3. Ask Reiki to flow through you and **into the family line**—to wherever healing is needed.
4. Use this intention:

   "I release the pain that no longer needs to be carried. I bless the strength that survives. I choose freedom—for myself and those who came before me."

Just for today, I will let go of worry and trust the flow of life.

5. End by thanking your ancestors and grounding them back into the present.

Reflection Prompts:

"What in me might have started before me?"
"What trauma am I willing to no longer carry forward?"
"What ancestral strength is ready to rise in me now?"

The "Inherited Belief Systems" Loop

Not all karma shows up as trauma or physical symptoms. Much of what we carry is more subtle, woven into the **beliefs we live by without questioning**. These beliefs—about ourselves, the world, and what's possible—are often inherited, not chosen. Passed down through generations like family heirlooms, they form energetic loops that keep us repeating patterns until we become conscious enough to break them.

This is the **Inherited Belief Systems Loop**—a karmic cycle created by internalized family, cultural, or societal conditioning that's rarely examined but constantly lived.

How Beliefs Become Energy Loops

When a belief is passed down (spoken or unspoken), and emotionally reinforced, it embeds itself into the **emotional body and subconscious mind**. These beliefs begin to shape:

- Your identity
- Your ability to receive love, abundance, or health
- Your perception of what's "safe" or "true"
- Your relationships and decision-making patterns

Belief becomes emotion. Emotion becomes frequency. Frequency attracts experience. And the loop continues.

Just for today, I will let go of worry and trust the flow of life.

Examples of Inherited Beliefs That Create Loops

- "Our family always struggles."
- "Love always leads to pain."
- "We don't talk about our feelings."
- "Men are supposed to be strong and silent."
- "Women in this family sacrifice for everyone else."
- "If you succeed, others will suffer."
- "Spiritual gifts are dangerous or shameful."
- "You must work hard to prove your worth."

These beliefs may not even be said out loud—but they are **felt, modeled, and absorbed** by children energetically, and they pass silently through the generations.

How to Recognize an Inherited Belief System Loop

- You find yourself repeating the same outcomes despite personal work.
- You feel guilt or fear when you try to change or grow.
- You self-sabotage after success or moments of joy.
- You feel "disloyal" or unsafe when stepping away from family norms.
- You hear internal voices that sound like your parents, grandparents, or cultural messages.
- You experience body tension, nausea, or guilt when trying to shift your story.

Breaking the Loop with Reiki + Awareness

Reiki helps disrupt the energetic charge of a limiting belief. When you bring loving energy and attention to the subconscious belief system, you begin to **soften the emotional charge**, which is what keeps it in place.

Steps to begin:

1. **Identify the belief** that feels inherited, not chosen.
2. **Ask where you feel it in your body** (solar plexus and heart are common).
3. Place your hands on that area and send Reiki.
4. Use the *I Forgives* technique to release emotional ties:

    "I forgive myself for believing I had to carry this belief to belong."
    "I forgive my family for teaching me limitation—they were surviving the best way they knew how."

5. Speak a new belief while Reiki flows:

    "It is safe to live by my own truth."
    "I bless my lineage by evolving."

Reflection Prompts:

"Whose voice lives inside my beliefs?"
"What patterns or messages did I absorb that limit me today?"
"Am I ready to release the need to repeat this for the sake of loyalty or safety?"

Just for today, I will let go of worry and trust the flow of life.

Healing with Reiki and Ancestral Altars

Bridging the Seen and Unseen

Creating an **ancestral altar** is a sacred way to honor your lineage, call in spiritual support, and provide a focused space for Reiki to flow through your family line. When combined with Reiki, an altar becomes a **portal of remembrance, forgiveness, and energetic restoration**—a living link between you and those who came before you.

Reiki helps transmute grief, pain, shame, and forgotten wisdom stored in your ancestral field. The altar acts as a **container for that healing**, offering reverence, structure, and soul presence.

Why Work with Ancestral Altars?

- To honor and reconnect with your roots—bloodline and spiritual
- To initiate healing for those who couldn't heal themselves
- To invite forward ancestral gifts, not just wounds
- To receive guidance, blessings, and messages
- To transform family trauma into strength and clarity

Many cultures have long practiced ancestor reverence. Whether or not you know your family history, working with an altar invites **healing beyond time and DNA**—especially when combined with Reiki's gentle power.

How to Create an Ancestral Altar

Start simple. Let your heart guide you. This is not about perfection—it's about presence.

Location:

Choose a quiet, sacred space in your home. A corner of a shelf, small table, or dedicated space works well.

Suggested Items:

- **Photos** of family members or symbolic representations (even just names written on paper)
- **Candles** to represent light, transformation, and guidance
- **Crystals** like black tourmaline, obsidian, or clear quartz for grounding and clarity
- **Natural elements** (flowers, water, soil, herbs) to represent the earth and lineage
- **Offerings** such as fruit, incense, tea, or food to symbolically nourish the ancestors
- **Reiki symbols** written or drawn, placed beneath or behind altar objects

Reiki Ancestral Altar Ritual

1. **Ground and Center**
   Sit before the altar. Place your hands over your heart or root chakra. Activate Reiki.
2. **Connect with Your Lineage**
   Say aloud or silently:

Just for today, I will let go of worry and trust the flow of life.

"I welcome the healed and healing ancestors into this space. I honor those known and unknown, and I offer this light in service of love and peace."

3. **Channel Reiki to the Line**
   Imagine Reiki flowing from your hands into the altar, then out through your family tree—both backward and forward in time. Let it reach the places that need healing, peace, or closure.
4. **Use "I Forgives" Statements**
   Speak healing intentions:
   o "I forgive the silence."
   o "I forgive the fear passed down."
   o "I allow myself to receive the wisdom that was hidden."
   o "I am safe to break the pattern and remain in love."
5. **Close in Gratitude**
   Offer thanks to your ancestors and to the Reiki energy. Blow out the candle or let it burn in a safe space. Leave offerings for a full day if desired.

You Can Return Often

You don't need to use the altar every day—but returning to it during healing sessions, family events, holidays, or emotional triggers can be deeply stabilizing. It becomes a space of both *release and remembrance.*

Reflection Prompts:

"What pain might my family have been carrying that was never spoken aloud?"
"What blessing or gift might I be the one to restore?"
"How can I be the bridge between the past and future generations?"

Just for today, I will let go of worry and trust the flow of life.

Clearing Family Cords and Vows

Releasing Energetic Ties from Generational Agreements

Some of the most persistent emotional patterns and spiritual blocks we carry aren't just inherited—they're **bound by energetic cords and unspoken vows**. These are unseen threads that connect us to family members, ancestral pain, outdated identities, or survival-based promises made long ago. While some cords represent love and support, others represent **entanglements that prevent soul-level freedom**.

Reiki, combined with intention, visualization, and forgiveness practices, offers a gentle yet powerful way to **release these energetic ties—not by cutting them—but by pulling them out at the root or dissolving them completely**, so that nothing is left to regrow.

What Are Family Cords?

Family cords are **energetic attachments** formed between you and members of your lineage. They may be rooted in love, protection, grief, guilt, responsibility, or even spiritual contracts. While some cords are healthy, others:

- Drain your energy
- Trigger repeating emotional responses
- Keep you "stuck" in patterns not meant for you
- Impose roles like "the healer," "the rescuer," or "the black sheep" of the family

These cords often attach at the **sacral, solar plexus, and heart chakras**, affecting your emotional balance, self-worth, and ability to individuate.

What Are Ancestral Vows?

Ancestral vows are **unconscious agreements** passed through generations or made by your soul in a past life. Examples include:

- "I'll carry the pain so others don't have to."
- "We don't talk about emotions in this family."
- "I must suffer to stay loyal to my ancestors."
- "We never leave each other, no matter what."
- "It's dangerous to be seen."

Though originally meant to protect, these vows can become energetic cages, keeping you tied to outdated belief systems, unhealthy dynamics, or ancestral trauma.

Reiki-Based Cord and Vow Clearing Process

This ritual can be done alone or with a practitioner. Always begin by grounding and activating Reiki.

Step-by-Step Practice: Dissolving Cords and Vows

1. **Set the Intention**

   "I am ready to dissolve any cords or vows inherited through my family line that no longer serve my soul's evolution."

Just for today, I will let go of worry and trust the flow of life.

2. **Scan the Body**
   Place your hands gently over your **solar plexus, sacral, or heart**. Ask:

   "Where in my body do I feel an energetic attachment that's not mine?"
   Notice any sensations—tightness, tingling, emotion.

3. **Call in the Cord**
   Visualize the cord: What does it look like? Where does it connect?
   Ask yourself or your guides:

   "What is this cord about? What belief or vow holds it in place?"

4. **Apply Reiki + I Forgives**
   As you hold the area, speak or think:
   - o "I forgive myself for believing I had to carry this."
   - o "I forgive the person or energy connected to this cord."
   - o "I release this with love for the highest good of all."
     Then visualize the cord **dissolving completely**—not cut, but gently unraveled and returned to Source.

5. **Replace with Light and Truth**
   Fill the space with Reiki and speak a new truth:

   "I am free to live by my own soul's wisdom."
   "I am loyal to love, not pain."

6. **Seal and Ground**
   Visualize your aura being sealed with golden light.
   Place your hands over your root chakra to ground.
   Drink water and journal afterward.

Important Note:

This process may bring up emotions, memories, or resistance. That's okay. Let Reiki guide the release gently. Never force it. You are never removing love—only **releasing outdated contracts or distortions** of love.

Reflection Prompts:

"What family role have I unconsciously accepted?"
"What agreements may I have made to stay small, silent, or suffering?"
"Am I ready to release loyalty to pain in exchange for loyalty to truth?"

Just for today, I will let go of worry and trust the flow of life.

Client Exercise: Timeline of the Family Wound

Mapping the Pattern So It Can Be Healed

Understanding where a family wound begins—and how it's evolved over time—is a powerful step in breaking its hold. This exercise allows clients (or yourself as the practitioner) to visually and intuitively **track a recurring pattern through generations**, identifying not just when it started but how it shifted, silenced, or survived.

The Timeline of the Family Wound gives shape to the invisible—bringing emotional clarity and ancestral perspective to karmic healing work.

Purpose of This Exercise

- To uncover the **origin of an emotional, behavioral, or energetic pattern**
- To recognize how it was passed down through stories, behaviors, silence, or trauma
- To develop compassion for the lineage—without carrying the wound forward
- To prepare for deeper clearing techniques like *I Forgives*, ancestral altar work, or vow/cord release

Before You Begin

Ground yourself. Activate Reiki. Place your hands over your heart or root chakra and set the intention:

"I am willing to see this pattern clearly, with love and without blame. I call on Reiki to guide my awareness and bring truth forward for healing."

Have paper and pen ready, or use a journal or worksheet designed for this purpose.

Instructions: Building Your Family Wound Timeline

Step 1: Name the Pattern
Choose one repeating pattern in your life or family line. Examples:

- Abandonment
- Suppressed emotions
- Financial instability
- Betrayal
- Abuse
- Sacrificing personal needs
- Being the emotional caretaker

Write it clearly at the top of your page:

"The Wound: Generational Silence Around Grief"

Step 2: Go Back as Far as You Can
Draw a timeline across your page. Start with your **great-grandparents or earliest known ancestors** and move forward through:

- Grandparents
- Parents
- You

Just for today, I will let go of worry and trust the flow of life.

- Your children (if applicable)

Leave space under each generation to add details.

Step 3: Record Known or Intuited Information
Under each generation, reflect:

- Who in this generation carried this pattern?
- What stories, behaviors, or events reflect it?
- What emotion seems to be at the root (fear, guilt, shame, resentment)?
- If unknown, ask Reiki or your intuition to guide insight.

You might recall a dream or a family story or have a "knowing" arise—trust it.

Step 4: How Did the Pattern Evolve?
Note whether the pattern:

- Grew stronger
- Became hidden
- Changed form (e.g., from alcohol to workaholism, or physical abuse to emotional detachment)

This helps show the **survival mechanism** behind the wound, which brings compassion and clarity.

Step 5: Identify the Turning Point
Ask:

- Where do I see the *invitation to heal*?

- Was there a family member who tried to change the pattern?
- Am I that turning point?

Circle your name or theirs.

Step 6: Reflection & Reiki Integration
Place your hands on your heart or solar plexus. Ask Reiki to flow through the entire timeline, bringing peace and light.

Repeat:

"I see the wound, and I choose to heal. I release the weight that isn't mine. I carry only the love forward."

Journal any insights, emotions, or resistance that came up.

Reflection Prompts:

"What is the core wound my family has carried?"
"Where did it begin, and how has it affected us emotionally?"
"What would it mean for me to break this cycle—and bless the lineage by doing so?"

Just for today, I will let go of worry and trust the flow of life.

PART 4:
ACCESSING THE
AKASHIC RECORDS

Chapter 4: Accessing the Akashic

What Are the Akashic Records?

The Akashic Records are often described as the **"Library of the Soul."** They are a vibrational archive of every soul's journey—across time, space, lifetimes, and dimensions. These records contain **every thought, emotion, action, and intention** your soul has ever experienced, including karmic patterns, soul contracts, and lessons in progress.

In Sanskrit, *Akasha* means "ether" or "spirit"—the element that holds all things. The Akashic Records are **not stored in a physical place** but within this energetic field. They exist as a **dimension of consciousness**, accessible through intention, intuition, and energy alignment.

Imagine the Akashic Records as a vast, luminous network of soul blueprints—each thread pulsing with memory, purpose, and potential.

Why Access the Akashic Records?

- To understand **why certain patterns** or relationships keep repeating
- To uncover **soul lessons** and karmic threads from past lives

Just for today, I will let go of worry and trust the flow of life.

- To explore **soul gifts** and latent abilities
- To receive guidance from your **Higher Self and spiritual team**
- To identify and release **contracts, vows, or blocks** keeping you from your purpose

Accessing these records isn't about prediction—it's about **clarity, healing, and transformation** at the soul level.

What You Might Find in the Records

- Key past lives impacting your current experience
- Karmic contracts or spiritual agreements still in effect
- Soul relationships (e.g., twin flames, karmic ties, soul family roles)
- Emotional residues or unhealed trauma
- Hidden talents, soul missions, and multidimensional experiences
- Vows (e.g., poverty, silence, suffering) ready to be released

Each session offers what the soul is **ready to receive**—no more, no less.

How Are the Records Accessed?

You do **not** need a specific lineage or religious training to access your own records. Many people open the Akashic field through:

- **Meditation and breathwork**
- **Spoken prayer or invocation**
- **Reiki energy flow**

- Sacred intention + intuitive guidance
- Working with trained Akashic Record readers

Because Reiki moves through the same Universal Life Force energy, it can serve as a gentle gateway to the Akashic field— especially when used with grounding and protection.

What It Feels Like to Enter the Records

People describe it as:

- A feeling of **deep peace and knowing**
- Receiving images, phrases, or full soul stories
- A subtle shift in vibration, like being held in light
- Emotions or memories surfacing with clarity or purpose
- A profound sense of **unconditional love and acceptance**

Some receive vivid visions. Others feel waves of insight. Even silence can be a powerful form of soul communication.

The records speak in the language of your intuition: images, symbols, emotions, knowing.

Reflection Prompts:

"What pattern in my life feels too deep to explain?"
"What wisdom might my soul already know that I've forgotten?"
"Am I ready to receive truth—even if it challenges what I thought I knew?"

Just for today, I will let go of worry and trust the flow of life.

Preparing with Reiki and Forgiveness

Clearing the Heart Before Entering the Records

The Akashic Records are not just an archive—they are a sacred space vibrating with **truth, compassion, and higher wisdom**. To enter them clearly and safely it helps to prepare your energetic field by releasing judgment, softening resistance, and aligning your heart with trust and humility.

One of the most powerful ways to prepare is through **Reiki and forgiveness**. Reiki harmonizes the body and aura, while forgiveness releases an emotional charge, clears karmic noise, and opens the soul to receive guidance from a place of love rather than fear or need.

Why Preparation Matters

- Unforgiven wounds can distort what you perceive in the records
- Holding onto guilt, blame, or shame creates **emotional static** that blocks clear reception
- When your heart is heavy, it's harder to recognize the soul's light and truth
- Forgiveness helps you **approach the Akashic field with reverence, neutrality, and grace**

The more you clear before you enter, the more clearly you can hear what's waiting for you.

Reiki + Forgiveness Preparation Ritual

Do this anytime before a session to center, clear, and prepare your energy field.

Step 1: Ground and Activate Reiki

- Sit or lie comfortably.
- Place your hands over your heart or solar plexus.
- Say aloud or silently:

  "I invite Reiki to flow through me, clearing what no longer serves and preparing me to enter the Akashic field in truth, humility, and love."

- Let the energy move through your body for several minutes. Breathe deeply.

Step 2: Use "I Forgives" for Emotional Clearing

Bring to mind anything or anyone you're holding judgment toward—including yourself. Speak these phrases aloud, or write them in your journal:

- "I forgive myself for not knowing."
- "I forgive myself for believing I was unworthy of truth or guidance."
- "I forgive anyone I've blamed for my pain or confusion."
- "I allow those I've harmed—intentionally or unintentionally—to forgive me."
- "I release the need to be right. I choose to be open."

Just for today, I will let go of worry and trust the flow of life.

Let Reiki flow to any part of your body that responds emotionally. Stay here as long as needed.

Step 3: Invite Alignment

Place one hand on your heart and one on your crown.

Say:

"I am open to truth beyond ego. I welcome insight without fear. I call forward only that which is in alignment with my highest path and purpose."

Optional Additions:

- Light a candle or place a crystal (amethyst, selenite, or clear quartz) nearby
- Journal a short intention:

  "Today, I open my records to understand…"

- Use a brief breath mantra:

  "Inhale peace… Exhale doubt."

Reflection Prompts:

"What emotion or belief might block me from receiving soul-level truth?"
"Who or what do I need to forgive before I step into the records?"
"Am I willing to hear what my soul is ready to share—even if it challenges my story?"

Preparing a Client with Reiki and Forgiveness

A Practitioner's Guide to Energetic Readiness Before an Akashic Session

When guiding a client into the Akashic Records—whether through Reiki, intuitive reading, or regression—it's essential to support their **emotional and energetic readiness** first. Clients often bring unconscious resistance, fear, or emotional debris that can distort what comes through.

By combining Reiki with a gentle forgiveness process, you can help them clear that static, center into the heart, and open to their soul's wisdom from a place of truth, safety, and compassion.

Step 1: Ground and Open the Space

- Begin the session by **clearing the room energetically** (smoke, sound, symbols, or Reiki).
- Ask the client to **sit or lie comfortably**, feet flat or body supported.
- Invite them to take 3 slow, grounding breaths while you place your hands on:
    - The **shoulders** (for grounding), or
    - The **heart and solar plexus** (for emotional balance)

Just for today, I will let go of worry and trust the flow of life.

Say:

"We begin by creating sacred space. I invite Reiki to flow through both of us, creating harmony and safety as we prepare to access your soul's truth."

Step 2: Scan the Emotional Field with Reiki

With your hands hovering or lightly placed, scan:

- The **solar plexus** for stored fear or control
- The **heart chakra** for grief, heartbreak, or guardedness
- The **throat chakra** for blocked expression or inner doubt

As you do, gently say:

"I'm inviting Reiki to show us if there's anything your soul is ready to release today—especially anything that could block or distort the messages waiting for you."

Take note of any emotional shifts, body movements, or intuitive nudges.

Step 3: Guide the Forgiveness Process (I Forgives Style)

Offer a few guided affirmations. You can speak them slowly and invite the client to repeat them silently or aloud.

Examples:

- "I forgive myself for what I didn't understand."
- "I forgive those who could not love, support, or guide me the way I needed."

- "I allow myself to forgive those I judged... and those who judged me."
- "I release the belief that I'm not worthy of accessing my truth."
- "I allow my ancestors and soul family to forgive me— for growing, for evolving, for letting go."

Pause and let Reiki flow during emotional moments. You may wish to place your hand over their **heart chakra** or **third eye** to help transmute grief or release.

Step 4: Seal the Preparation with Intention

Ask the client to place one hand on their heart and one on their lower belly (or do so for them gently).

Speak this invocation:

"I am open to receiving what my soul is ready to reveal. I welcome truth, not from the mind, but from the highest vibration of love and clarity. I now open to the wisdom within the Akashic Field."

Let Reiki flow for 1–3 more minutes in silence, allowing the energy to stabilize and integrate.

Optional Enhancements:

- Light a candle or use an essential oil (like frankincense, lavender, or palo santo)
- Use crystals such as **celestite, amethyst, or selenite** on or near the client

Just for today, I will let go of worry and trust the flow of life.

- Ask the client to journal a single question or intention for their Akashic session

Reflection Questions for Debrief (Post-Access):

"How did your energy shift during the forgiveness process?"
"What did you feel opening in your body as we began the Reiki?"
"Was there a particular moment that softened or surprised you?"

Symbolic Language of the Soul Library

How the Akashic Records Speak Through Symbols, Emotions, and Intuition

The Akashic Records don't speak in spoken words or written sentences. Instead, they communicate through a **symbolic language uniquely tailored to each soul**—a blend of emotions, imagery, intuitive downloads, and metaphors. This "soul language" can feel subtle or surreal at first, but with practice and presence, it becomes clear and unmistakable.

Understanding the symbolic language of the Records is essential for interpreting what's shown during a Reiki-Akashic session—whether for yourself or your clients.

Why the Records Speak in Symbols

Your soul exists beyond the limits of linear time, spoken language, or human logic. Symbols are **universal, timeless, and emotionally resonant**, making them the perfect medium for:

- Delivering multi-layered truths
- Activating memories across lifetimes
- Revealing soul contracts, wounds, or gifts
- Offering healing in a way your subconscious can integrate

Symbols carry energy and meaning **specific to your personal and soul history**, even if they seem strange or abstract in the moment.

Just for today, I will let go of worry and trust the flow of life.

How the Soul Speaks Through the Akashic Field

You may receive:

- **Images** (e.g., a door, a staircase, a flame)
- **Sensations** (tightness, warmth, vibration)
- **Emotions** (waves of grief, peace, fear, or awe)
- **Colors or light**
- **Sounds or tones**
- **Single words or short messages**
- **Repetitive motifs** (e.g., birds, mountains, locked boxes)

These symbols are not distractions—they are the message.

Examples of Common Symbols and Their Meanings

Symbol	Possible Meaning
A locked door	Blocked truth or soul memory
A staircase	Ascension, spiritual growth, or next-level soul work
Water	Emotional flow, healing, unresolved grief
Fire	Purification, transformation, power awakening
Mirror	Identity, self-reflection, karmic echo
Bridge	Transition between lives, relationships, or timelines

Symbol	Possible Meaning
Scroll or book	Soul contract or purpose being revealed
Child	Inner child, past life as a child, rebirth
Animal guide	A soul ally or message about survival, instinct, or freedom

Remember: Your **personal associations** with a symbol matter more than any universal definition.

How to Interpret Symbols in a Reiki-Akashic Session

1. **Stay present with the first impression.**
   Don't overthink it. The first image or emotion that arises is often the truth your soul is showing you.
2. **Ask the symbol questions.**

   "What do you want me to know?"
   "Where in my life does this show up?"
   "How is this related to my current pattern or healing?"

3. **Feel it, don't fix it.**
   Let Reiki move through the symbol. Observe how your body or energy field responds—this tells you where the symbol is held in your emotional body.
4. **Journal and revisit.**
   Sometimes the meaning of a symbol reveals itself over days. Keep notes and allow the insight to unfold.

Just for today, I will let go of worry and trust the flow of life.

Reflection Prompts:

"What symbol or image stood out most in my session?"
"Did it evoke a memory, a feeling, or a knowing?"
"Where might this message apply in my current life, pattern, or healing?"
"Am I willing to trust my soul's language—even if I don't fully understand it yet?"

Crafting the Right Questions to Ask

How to Open the Akashic Records With Clarity, Curiosity, and Purpose

When entering the Akashic Records—whether for yourself or a client—the energy responds not just to your intention but to the **questions you ask**. Clear, well-crafted questions act as tuning forks, helping you **align with specific frequencies of truth, healing, or soul insight.**

Vague or fear-based questions often lead to confusion, emotional overwhelm, or empty space. Empowering, open-hearted questions, on the other hand, open the Records like a flower—revealing depth, meaning, and guidance beyond what the conscious mind could reach.

Why Questions Matter

In the Akashic Field:

- You receive what you're *ready* to hear
- The more specific and open your question, the more direct the response
- The Records are not predictive—they are reflective
- Avoid asking "yes/no" or "should I" questions—they limit your access to truth

Instead, use questions that begin with:

- **What…**
- **How…**

Just for today, I will let go of worry and trust the flow of life.

- **Why…** (with care and readiness)
- **What is the soul lesson…**
- **What am I being invited to see…**

Examples of Soul-Aligned Questions

For Emotional or Relationship Healing:

- "What past life or ancestral pattern is influencing this relationship dynamic?"
- "What is the deeper soul contract between me and this person?"
- "What am I being asked to learn, heal, or release through this connection?"

For Karmic Pattern Clarity:

- "What repeating pattern am I ready to break?"
- "Where did this belief/emotion originate in my soul's timeline?"
- "What energy have I been carrying that is no longer mine to hold?"

For Purpose and Life Direction:

- "What soul gifts am I being invited to reclaim now?"
- "What is blocking me from stepping into my purpose?"
- "What is the next aligned step on my path of service or healing?"

For Ancestral Healing:

- "What family belief or wound am I here to transform?"
- "What ancestral energy is affecting this area of my life?"
- "How can I bring healing to my lineage through this situation?"

For Personal Evolution:

- "What do I need to remember about my soul's truth in this moment?"
- "What energy or vow is keeping me from receiving love/abundance/peace?"
- "What would it feel like to fully align with my higher self?"

Tips for Practitioners Guiding Clients

- **Have your client write or speak their question beforehand**
- Help them shift from fear-based phrasing ("Why does this always happen to me?") to empowerment ("What is the deeper lesson my soul is revealing?")
- **Write down their core questions before opening the records** so you can hold focus when energy starts to flow
- **Encourage emotional neutrality**—the Records respond to openness, not expectation

Just for today, I will let go of worry and trust the flow of life.

Reflection Prompts:

"What question has been sitting in my heart for a long time?"
"What do I truly want to understand about myself beyond the surface?"
"If I had the courage to know the truth, what would I ask?"

The Role of Intuition: Claircognizance, Clairvoyance, and Clairsentience

How Your Soul Receives Truth from the Akashic Field

When you access the Akashic Records—whether for yourself or as a practitioner—you are not "reading" in the traditional sense. You are receiving. And the way you receive is through **your intuitive channels**, also known as the *"clairs."*

Understanding how your intuition works allows you to **trust the information that comes through**, interpret it accurately, and guide others more clearly. Everyone has intuitive ability—but most people naturally lean toward one or two dominant senses. In the Akashic field, these intuitive senses become the **language through which soul memory speaks**.

The 3 Primary Clairs in Akashic Work

1. Claircognizance – "Clear Knowing"

This is the **gut sense or inner knowing** that arrives without explanation. You may not see or hear anything—but you suddenly *know* what the message is.

- Feels like a direct download or deep certainty
- Often instantaneous, bypassing logic
- You may say, "I don't know how I know, I just do."
- Common in Reiki practitioners, teachers, and healers who "channel" words, insight, or answers

Just for today, I will let go of worry and trust the flow of life.

In the Akashic Records, this may show up as:

A flash of truth, a phrase that repeats in your mind, or the knowing of a soul lesson before you see or feel it.

2. Clairvoyance – "Clear Seeing"

Clairvoyants receive insight through **visual imagery**—this could be a vivid picture, symbol, flash of a past life scene, color, or metaphor.

- It may look like a movie playing behind the eyes
- Sometimes seen in the "mind's eye" or third eye
- Includes dreams, visions, light flashes, or symbolic imagery
- Often linked with soul memories, symbols, and archetypes

In the Akashic Records, this may show up as:

Seeing yourself in a different body or time period, noticing symbolic objects (scrolls, doors, staircases), or visions of energy cords or soul contracts.

3. Clairsentience – "Clear Feeling"

Clairsentients receive through **body-based emotion and sensation**. You may physically feel the energy of the message in your chest, stomach, throat, or hands.

- Emotions surface suddenly and strongly
- Physical sensations may include warmth, chills, tightness, or pressure

- Often accompanied by empathy, grief release, or emotional waves
- Very common in past life regression and ancestral healing work

In the Akashic Records, this may show up as:

Feeling what a past version of you felt during a trauma, sensing a loved one's pain, or absorbing ancestral grief or strength.

Bonus: Other Clair Senses

While Claircognizance, Clairvoyance, and Clairsentience are the most common in Akashic work, you may also experience:

- **Clairaudience** – hearing words, names, or tones in your inner ear
- **Clairalience** – smelling something associated with a soul memory (e.g., smoke, perfume)
- **Clairgustance** – tasting something that connects you to a person, life, or event

How to Strengthen Your Intuitive Channel

- Spend time in silence before and after Akashic work
- Journal every impression, no matter how small
- Let go of needing to "get it right"—intuition deepens with trust
- Use Reiki to activate the **third eye, crown, and heart chakras**

Just for today, I will let go of worry and trust the flow of life.

- Practice: "If I *did* trust this message, what would it mean to me?"

Reflection Prompts:

"Which clair do I naturally use most often?"
"When I receive intuitive information, how does it arrive?"
"How can I support my intuitive gifts as a language of soul connection?"

Referenced Verse: 1 Corinthians 12 – The Nine Gifts of the Spirit

Honoring the Spiritual Foundation of Intuitive and Healing Gifts

At the heart of energy healing and soul remembrance lies the recognition that **our gifts are not random—they are sacred**. Whether you call them abilities, talents, sensitivities, or "clairs," these gifts are part of a divine blueprint encoded into your soul. Many spiritual traditions reference this truth, but one of the most well-known is found in the **Bible—1 Corinthians, Chapter 12**.

This passage lists **Nine Spiritual Gifts** given by the Spirit—not based on merit but as a **divine calling to serve, uplift, and heal.** These gifts mirror many of the intuitive and energetic abilities we explore through Reiki, Akashic Record work, and karmic healing.

1 Corinthians 12:7–11 (NIV)

"Now to each one, the manifestation of the Spirit is given for the common good. To one there is given through the Spirit the message of wisdom, to another the message of knowledge by means of the same Spirit, to another faith by the same Spirit, to another gifts of healing by that one Spirit, to another miraculous powers, to another prophecy, to another distinguishing between spirits, to another speaking in different kinds of tongues, and to still another the interpretation of tongues."

Just for today, I will let go of worry and trust the flow of life.

The Nine Gifts Listed in the Verse:

1. **Word of Wisdom** – The ability to access divine insight and guidance beyond the mind
2. **Word of Knowledge** – Intuitive understanding of truth without prior learning
3. **Faith** – The unshakable belief in divine will, healing, and miracles
4. **Gifts of Healing** – Spiritual and energetic healing of the body, mind, or soul
5. **Miraculous Powers** – The ability to manifest or shift energy in ways that transcend logic
6. **Prophecy** – Clear vision of future potential, soul messages, or divine warnings
7. **Discernment of Spirits** – Knowing what energy or spirit is present and its intent
8. **Speaking in Tongues** – Spiritual language or vibrational communication beyond human speech
9. **Interpretation of Tongues** – The ability to understand and interpret divine or energetic language

Why This Verse Matters in Karmic & Intuitive Healing

Whether you're religious, spiritual, or energetically attuned, this passage reminds us that:

- We are **meant to remember and use our gifts**
- These gifts are **not ego-driven**, but **service-oriented**
- All spiritual abilities are **equal in value and purpose**
- We are each entrusted with a unique combination of healing frequencies

Reflection Prompts:

"Which of these gifts do I feel called to explore or reclaim?"
"How might I have used these gifts in a past life?"
"What healing work am I being called to do with my gifts in this lifetime?"

Just for today, I will let go of worry and trust the flow of life.

PART 5.
KARMIC CONTRACTS,
SOUL AGREEMENTS, AND
SPIRITUAL LOOPS

Chapter 5: Karmic Contracts, Soul Agreements, and Spiritual Earth stands behind you,

Karmic Contracts, Soul Agreements, and Spiritual Loops
Soul Contracts – What Are They Really?

At the heart of our soul's journey are **agreements made before incarnation**—contracts we willingly enter into to learn, grow, evolve, and heal. These **soul contracts** are not punishments, but rather sacred commitments designed to help us remember who we are and what we came here to experience.

Unlike legal contracts, soul contracts are **energetic and spiritual in nature**. They may be made:

- Between two or more souls
- Between the soul and the Universe or divine plan
- Between the soul and its own higher purpose

They often involve *growth through contrast*—meaning we may choose to experience challenge, resistance, or pain as a **catalyst** for soul evolution.

Just for today, I will let go of worry and trust the flow of life.

How Soul Contracts Are Created

Before birth, your soul meets with **guides, teachers, and soul companions** to plan major themes of your life:

- What lessons will be explored
- What karmic patterns may arise
- Who will help you awaken (often through both love and conflict)
- What spiritual gifts or service you are here to share

These contracts may involve:

- Family relationships
- Friendships and soulmates
- Trauma or healing events
- Past life karmic resolution
- A specific mission or calling

We choose the souls we grow with—not for ease, but for evolution.

Why We Forget Our Contracts

Part of the soul contract includes **the veil of forgetting**. We are born into human form with amnesia, allowing us to rediscover our power, remember our truth, and reclaim our gifts through lived experience.

If we knew all the answers, we wouldn't grow into the versions of ourselves who could embody them.

This forgetting is not failure—it's **spiritual design**.

Soul Contracts vs. Karmic Debt

While some contracts are based in **love and support**, others arise from **unresolved energy** from past lives—what we might call karmic debt. These contracts help bring:

- Closure to a story left unfinished
- Healing to a wound that remains open
- Balance to energy that was once misused or denied

But it's important to remember:
Karma is not punishment.
It is simply the energetic consequence of past choices and the opportunity to realign with truth.

Signs You're In a Soul Contract

- You feel **intensely drawn** to someone, even if they challenge or hurt you
- A relationship triggers deep emotional patterns—but keeps returning
- You can't seem to "move on" until you've learned something from the experience
- You sense you've known someone for lifetimes
- You feel bound to a situation despite efforts to leave it
- You hear yourself say things like:

"I know this is hard… but it feels like something I agreed to."

Just for today, I will let go of worry and trust the flow of life.

Can Soul Contracts Be Broken or Completed?

Yes—when the lesson is learned, the energy integrated, and the forgiveness offered, the contract is either fulfilled or dissolved. You don't have to stay in suffering to be loyal to a spiritual agreement. Many soul contracts are complete once:

- You reclaim your power
- You choose love over fear
- You forgive the karmic entanglement
- You step into a new pattern of behavior or belief

Reiki and Akashic healing help clients recognize and release outdated contracts, especially when combined with the *I Forgives* technique and symbolic regression work.

Reflection Prompts:

"What experience or person in my life feels spiritually 'contracted'?"
"What might I have agreed to learn from this soul or situation?"
"Am I ready to honor the lesson and let the contract dissolve?"

How to Know You're in a Soul Contract or Karmic Loop

Recognizing the Signs of Spiritual Agreements Still in Motion

Many people are unaware they're living out a soul contract or karmic agreement—because these experiences often feel like ordinary struggles, relationships, or emotional challenges. But underneath the surface, a **spiritual loop is running**—inviting you to awaken, heal, and choose differently.

Recognizing that you're in a contract is the **first step to breaking the cycle.**

Key Signs You're In a Soul Contract or Karmic Loop

1. You Feel Stuck—No Matter What You Do

- You've tried therapy, coaching, energy work, affirmations… yet the same emotional pattern, situation, or relationship keeps repeating.
- The "lesson" seems just out of reach, like you're circling it but not integrating it.

2. There's a Magnetic Pull to Someone or Something

- You feel drawn to a person (or pushed by a situation) without logic or reason.
- You may feel love, anger, confusion, or guilt—but you *can't* let it go.
- It feels "fated" or destined, even if painful.

Just for today, I will let go of worry and trust the flow of life.

3. Your Body Reacts

- You get physical symptoms when you're around certain people or in specific roles (tightness in the chest, stomach knots, sudden fatigue).
- You sense energetic entanglement—even when apart.

4. There's an Unresolved Emotional Theme

- Guilt, betrayal, abandonment, unworthiness, sacrifice, or fear of speaking your truth are ongoing struggles in your life.
- These emotions often arise in key relationships—especially family, partners, or long-term friendships.

5. You Know Something Is Unspoken or Unfinished

- There's an intuitive feeling: *"This isn't just about this lifetime."*
- You've had dreams, visions, or past life memories related to the person or pattern.
- You might say, "It feels like we've done this before."

6. You Feel Bound by Loyalty or Obligation

- You can't walk away, even though the situation is draining or toxic.
- A part of you believes: *"If I leave, I'll fail them (or fail the soul contract)."*

7. Time Doesn't Change It

- Years may pass, but the emotional charge remains.
- New relationships mirror the same dynamic.
- Even distance doesn't dissolve the pattern.

Karmic Loop vs. Active Healing

You may be in a **loop** if:

- The same pattern keeps repeating without change
- You feel exhausted, emotionally depleted, or powerless
- You react the same way each time, even though you wish you wouldn't

You're likely **moving through a contract** when:

- You're becoming more aware of the pattern
- You're changing how you respond, even if it's hard
- You feel more empowered, clear, and emotionally free after each cycle

Reflection Prompts:

"What emotional pattern or relationship keeps showing up in my life?"
"What am I still trying to fix, prove, or redeem through this experience?"
"Does this feel bigger than me—like it spans lifetimes or generations?"

Just for today, I will let go of worry and trust the flow of life.

Reiki Cord-Removal and Soul Clearing

Dissolving Energetic Attachments at the Root—With Love and Finality

As we move through karmic healing, one of the most profound and necessary practices is **clearing the energetic cords** that bind us to the past—whether to people, events, ancestral lines, or unresolved soul contracts. These cords carry emotional energy, belief systems, and soul imprints that keep us connected to **outdated identities and unfinished lessons.**

But unlike many approaches that speak of "cutting" cords, in this Reiki Wisdom lineage, we believe:

We do not cut cords—we gently pull them out at the root or dissolve them completely.
This ensures that nothing is left behind to reattach or regrow from pain, fear, or memory.

What Are Energetic Cords?

Energetic cords are **invisible attachments** that connect us to others through the energy of:

- Guilt, shame, obligation
- Control, codependency, or trauma
- Past lives, ancestral lineage, or karmic vows
- Unforgiveness or emotional loops
- Even love that has turned heavy, possessive, or unresolved

These cords often anchor in the **chakras**—particularly the sacral, solar plexus, heart, and throat—and they can interfere with emotional sovereignty, energetic clarity, and forward movement.

Symptoms You May Need Cord Clearing

- You feel **drained** after being around a certain person
- You're constantly **thinking about someone**, even if you're no longer in contact
- You **can't move on** from a relationship, trauma, or belief
- You feel **tied** to family patterns or soul responsibilities that don't feel like yours
- You've done inner work, but the emotional charge **still lingers**

Reiki Soul Clearing and Cord Removal Process

This process can be done **on yourself or with a client**. Always begin by grounding, calling in protection, and activating Reiki.

Step-by-Step Cord Dissolution & Soul Clearing

1. Set the Intention

"I now choose to release any energetic cords, attachments, or imprints that no longer serve my soul's highest path. May they dissolve completely—with love, grace, and truth."

Just for today, I will let go of worry and trust the flow of life.

2. Scan the Energy Field

Using your hands or intuitive sensing, scan the body for areas of:

- Tightness
- Pulsing
- Coldness or numbness
- Emotional reaction

Focus especially on the **chakras** and solar plexus (power center).

3. Identify the Cord

Gently ask:

"Where is this cord attached?"
"What is the emotion or story it's holding?"
"Is this from this life, a past life, or ancestral?"

Let the imagery, emotions, or knowing arise. Trust what comes.

4. Channel Reiki Into the Corded Area

Place your hands over the area. Allow Reiki to flow, softening the bond. Visualize the cord becoming visible and slowly loosening from its anchor point.

5. Use the Release Invocation

As the Reiki flows, speak or guide the client to say:

"I release this cord and all its agreements. I dissolve its root, memory, and meaning across all time, space, and dimensions.

I bless the person or energy involved and reclaim my wholeness now."

6. Visualize the Cord Dissolving or Uprooting
See the cord:

- Unwinding like a root from the soil
- Melting into light
- Returning to Source in peace

Never cut. Always dissolve or uproot completely.

7. Fill the Space with Reiki and Truth
Place your hands over the cleared area and say:

"I fill this space with light, truth, and divine love. I call back all soul fragments and energy that belong to me—whole and healed."

8. Seal and Ground
Visualize a **golden seal of light** around the body. Run your hands down the aura to smooth and seal the field. Ground the energy through the root chakra.

Optional: Add a Ritual Element

- Write the cord's name or pattern on paper, then burn it
- Place a crystal (black tourmaline, selenite, or obsidian) over the release area
- Use essential oils like **frankincense, myrrh, or lemon** to energetically cleanse

Just for today, I will let go of worry and trust the flow of life.

Reflection Prompts:

"What did this cord teach me—and what am I now ready to reclaim?"

"What truth or emotion was buried beneath this attachment?"

"What do I feel now that the space is mine again?"

Emotional Detachment with Compassion

Letting Go Without Abandoning Love

In the process of karmic healing, ancestral release, and soul contract work, you will likely come to a point where you must **emotionally detach from someone or something**—not out of anger, resentment, or rejection—but from a **place of deep compassion and personal sovereignty.**

Detachment is not disconnection.
It is a conscious act of **energetic clarity** that allows you to love without losing yourself.

What Emotional Detachment Really Means

True detachment is not coldness or avoidance. It is the art of:

- Holding space for someone else's journey **without absorbing it**
- Releasing the belief that **you are responsible for their healing, emotions, or choices**
- Honoring your own energy while still offering love
- Letting go of outcomes while still wishing others well

Compassion says, "I love you."
Detachment says, "And I return to myself."

Just for today, I will let go of worry and trust the flow of life.

Why This Is Crucial in Karmic and Ancestral Healing

When we work through karmic contracts and generational trauma, we often come face to face with:

- Parents, partners, or ancestors who could not meet our needs
- Loved ones who continue to choose pain, silence, or denial
- Clients or family members who seek healing but resist change

Staying emotionally entangled can cause:

- Energy leaks
- Prolonged grief or guilt
- Blocked intuitive clarity
- Re-triggering of old wounds
- Reactivated cords and patterns, you've already released

Reiki Practice for Compassionate Detachment

1. Begin with the Heart
Place your hands over your heart. Activate Reiki. Say:

"I honor this connection, and I release the need to carry it."

2. Visualize the Person or Pattern in Light
Imagine them in their own sphere of light. See that they are not yours to save—they are sovereign, as are you.

3. Use a Compassionate Release Affirmation:

"I release this with love.
I allow you to walk your path, and I return to mine.
I am no longer attached through guilt, fear, or obligation."

4. Send Reiki to Yourself

Especially the heart and solar plexus. Invite in freedom, peace, and neutrality.

What Detachment Feels Like

- A sense of **calm clarity** even when the situation is unresolved
- The ability to witness another's pain **without absorbing it**
- Emotional boundaries with **open-heartedness**
- No longer trying to fix, chase, or prove
- A peaceful separation from patterns that once controlled you

You're not hard—you're healed.

Reflection Prompts:

"What emotional tie am I ready to release—but afraid it will seem like abandonment?"
"What would it feel like to love them **without entangling myself** in their pain?"
"Can I trust that releasing them is also a way of honoring their soul's freedom?"

Just for today, I will let go of worry and trust the flow of life.

PART 6:
FORGIVENESS AND
KARMIC FREEDOM

Chapter 6: Forgiveness and Karmic Freedom

Forgiveness and Karmic Freedom
Why Forgiveness is the Key to All Healing

Forgiveness is not a spiritual cliché—it is a **soul technology**.

It is the key that unlocks karmic cages. It is the light that dissolves energetic residue. It is the act that **frees you from loops of pain, blame, betrayal, and bondage.** Without forgiveness, no amount of energy work, regression, or cord-clearing can truly set you free—because the *emotional anchor* remains.

Forgiveness is not for the other person—it's for **your frequency, your freedom, and your future**.

The Karmic Cycle and the Role of Forgiveness

Karma often presents as a repeating emotional pattern:

- The same type of relationship… different person
- The same reaction… in different situations
- The same wound… playing out over generations

Each time the pattern reappears, it's a **soul invitation** to respond differently.

Just for today, I will let go of worry and trust the flow of life.

Forgiveness is that response.

When you forgive:

- You reclaim energy lost to the past
- You end the emotional charge tethering you to someone else's story
- You release your role in the karmic exchange
- You allow the cycle to complete without carrying it into future lives

Forgiveness is **how karma is dissolved.**

Forgiveness vs. Forgetting or Approving

Let's be clear:
Forgiveness is **not** forgetting.
It is **not** condoning.
It is **not** bypassing pain.

Forgiveness is the choice to:

- Stop rehearsing the pain in your energy field
- Acknowledge the wound and still choose peace
- Free yourself **and** the other person (even if they never change)

Energetic Consequences of Withholding Forgiveness

When you hold on to resentment, you:

- Keep your aura contracted
- Invite dis-ease or imbalance
- Block intuitive clarity and soul alignment

- Remain tied through invisible cords to the source of your pain

When you forgive, your vibration shifts—**instantly**. Reiki flows more easily. Akashic insight becomes clearer. Your nervous system relaxes. Your body heals. Your soul expands.

A Reiki-Based Forgiveness Practice

1. Place one hand over your heart and the other over your solar plexus.
2. Activate Reiki and say:

   "I am ready to forgive—not for them, but for me."

3. Breathe into the emotion. Let it rise. Let Reiki flow through it.
4. Speak what you're ready to release:

   "I forgive what happened."
   "I forgive what wasn't said or done."
   "I forgive the energy of the experience—even if I don't fully understand it."

Let tears fall. Let truth surface. Let the memory shift.

Reflection Prompts:

"What or who have I been unwilling to forgive—and what has that cost me?"
"What would I gain if I forgave fully?"
"Am I ready to stop holding this in my field and call my power back?"

Just for today, I will let go of worry and trust the flow of life.

Reiki Journey: The Maze of the Self

A Guided Visualization for Releasing Karmic Weight Through Forgiveness and Light

Inspired by the story "The Maze" from Fairytales, Dreams and Reality... Where Are You on Your Path?

How to Use This Practice

This journey can be read silently, recorded as a meditation, or guided for a client session. It's especially powerful after completing energy cord release or karmic clearing work.

Begin the Journey

Find a quiet, comfortable place where you can sit or lie down undisturbed. Close your eyes. Place your hands on your heart or solar plexus and activate Reiki. Take three slow, grounding breaths.

The Meditation

Now, imagine yourself standing at the entrance of a maze—not made of walls, but of soft, shimmering silk. The panels stretch high above you, translucent and glowing faintly in the light.

On your back is a **backpack**—heavy, though you're unsure why. It feels soft, but its weight pulls your shoulders low.

You hear a gentle voice within you say:

"Walk the path. Trust the weight. Learn from it. And when you're ready, release it."

You take your first step into the maze.

Immediately, you come to a barrier. The silk stretches in front of you—no clear way forward. You pause.

You notice the presence of others on the other side of the panels. You can see their shapes. You can hear their movement. But they are not walking your path.

You realize this maze is yours alone.

You sit down, breathing into the weight on your back. You wonder what it holds… and why it feels so heavy.

A quiet voice within you says:

"Look inside."

You take off the backpack and open it.

It's empty.

But as you lift it, the heaviness remains.

You feel the burden. And suddenly, you understand—it's not the bag. **It's you.** You are carrying memories, pain, resentment, guilt, and self-judgment. These unseen weights have formed in your energy field.

"I carry my past within me," you whisper. *"But I also have the power to set it down."*

Just for today, I will let go of worry and trust the flow of life.

Still holding the pack in your hands, you think of someone who hurt you—someone whose energy has stayed with you long after they've left your life.

You Speak aloud: **"I forgive you, wherever you are. I release the story. I choose peace."**

The pack lightens.

Next, you recall a time you disappointed yourself—when you acted from fear, shame, or pain.

You Say: **"I forgive myself for what I didn't yet know. I allow myself to grow and let go."**

The pack lightens again.

You begin to walk, and each time a wall appears, you pause and forgive:

- A parent
- A friend
- A version of yourself
- A belief that once kept you safe

With each forgiveness, the pack grows lighter… and so do you.

A warm light shines above the maze. You feel it touch your skin. It's not just sunlight—it's **Divine Love**. It sees you. It knows you. It radiates your true self.

You smile, and the last of the weight dissolves.

You no longer need to carry anything.

Your body lifts gently—first your heart, then your feet.
You rise above the silk panels, above the maze itself.

From this height, you see others still walking their own
paths—just as you once did. But you don't feel pity. You feel
compassion.

You whisper to them:

"When you are ready, you will forgive too. You will fly."

You float down gently, not to the beginning—but beyond
the maze.

Your path is clear now.

Place your hands again over your heart and say:

**"I am the light and the way. I carry healing within me.
Through forgiveness and love, I release my past. I am free. I
am whole. I am light."**

Breathe deeply.

Let Reiki continue to flow through you as long as needed.

When ready, gently open your eyes and return to the present
moment—lighter than before.

Just for today, I will let go of worry and trust the flow of life.

Integration Prompts:

"What weight was I ready to release today?"
"What part of me felt seen or healed?"
"Who or what do I now forgive so I may fly?"

The "I Forgives" Method: A 3-Step Holistic Technique

Emotional Alchemy Through Self-Awareness, Compassion, and Energetic Release

The **"I Forgives" Method** is a conscious, heart-centered process designed to create **true energetic freedom** through forgiveness. It's not just about saying the words—it's about **feeling the shift**, reclaiming your power, and **healing the charge** behind the wound.

Forgiveness through this method happens in **three layers**:

1. **Yourself**
2. **The Other**
3. **The Completion**—where you allow them to forgive you

Each step honors your experience, clears karmic imprints, and activates the heart field for transformation. Reiki supports the entire process by calming the nervous system and carrying your intention deep into the emotional and spiritual body.

Step 1: Forgive Yourself

This is the beginning of all healing. Forgiving yourself is not about excusing past decisions—it's about **freeing yourself from self-condemnation** and making space for growth.

Place your hands on your heart or solar plexus. Breathe deeply. Speak:

Just for today, I will let go of worry and trust the flow of life.

"I forgive myself for holding onto this pain longer than I needed to."
"I forgive myself for not knowing what I couldn't have known then."
"I allow myself to forgive myself for repeating this pattern."
"I forgive myself for betraying my own truth to please or protect others."
"I forgive myself for carrying this for so long—and I now let it go."

Let the words wash through you. Let the emotion rise and fall. Reiki will hold the rest.

Step 2: Forgive Others

Now, bring to mind the person, pattern, or presence that played a role in your pain. You're not saying what happened was okay—you're saying you're **no longer willing to carry the wound.**

This step is for your peace, not their approval.

With your hands placed where you feel the charge, say:

"I forgive _____ for the role they played in my life."
"I forgive _____ for what they did—or failed to do."
"I allow myself to release the emotional weight I've held toward them."
"I forgive them for being human, and I set myself free."

Let Reiki soften your edges. Allow space for resistance—it's part of the process.

Step 3: Allow Others to Forgive You

This is the often-overlooked part of the healing equation. When we evolve, it may activate guilt—even over actions we didn't mean to take. And sometimes, we carry invisible shame over simply choosing to break the cycle.

This final step honors your **soul sovereignty** and invites the **completion** of the karmic story.

Breathe gently. Place your hands over your root or heart. Speak:

"I allow _____ to forgive me for choosing to grow beyond the story we once shared."
"I allow _____ to forgive me for letting go, even if they never understand why."
"I allow those I've hurt—intentionally or unintentionally—to find peace with our past."
"I allow the bond between us to dissolve in light and love, for the highest good of all."

Feel the field shift. Let the final thread release. You are free now.

Closing Affirmation

"I have forgiven. I have been forgiven. I am free. I walk forward with love, grace, and clarity."

Just for today, I will let go of worry and trust the flow of life.

How to Know Which Step to Start With

(Client Intuition or Session Goal)

A Practitioner's Guide to Navigating the "I Forgives" Method in Real-Time

The beauty of the **I Forgives Method** lies in its flexibility—it honors the individual soul's timing, readiness, and inner knowing. While it's presented as a 3-step process (forgive yourself → forgive others → allow others to forgive you), healing is rarely linear. **Your client's energy field will tell you where to begin.**

This section helps you learn how to **intuitively assess which forgiveness step to start with**, whether in self-practice or client sessions.

Option 1: Let the Client's Intuition Lead

Before you begin any forgiveness process, ask:

"Where in your body do you feel this most?"
"What's the strongest emotion showing up right now?"
"Is the heaviness toward yourself, someone else, or the whole story?"

Clients often know without knowing. Their responses may point you directly to the **energetic starting point**:

Client Says...	Begin With...
"I should've known better..."	Forgive Self
"They never apologized for what they did."	Forgive Others
"I feel guilty for ending things."	Allow Them to Forgive You
"I keep reliving what I said/did."	Forgive Self
"I wish I could go back and fix it."	Forgive Self and Allow Forgiveness from Others
"They're the ones who caused this."	Forgive Others (then Self)

Let the conversation guide the energetic entry point. **Trust the first truth that surfaces.**

Option 2: *Use the Session's Goal to Determine Entry Point*

If the session has a clear intention (e.g., ancestral healing, past life release, relationship closure), you can guide the process based on **what's most relevant to the theme.**

Just for today, I will let go of worry and trust the flow of life.

Session Goal	Start With...
Releasing guilt, shame, self-sabotage	Forgive Self
Ending toxic cords or contracts	Forgive Others
Completing karmic lessons or vows	Allow Others to Forgive You
Moving forward after a breakup/divorce	All 3 (start with most charged)
Ancestral healing	Forgive Others → Allow Forgiveness → Forgive Self
Past life regression & closure	Follow emotional intensity from vision (usually Forgive Others first)

Reiki Tip: Use the Body as a Map

If a client doesn't know where to begin:

1. Activate Reiki.
2. Place one hand over the **heart chakra** and the other over the **solar plexus**.
3. Ask the client:

   "Which part feels heavier or more active?"
   "If this emotion had a voice, what would it say?"

Often:

- Heart = grief, betrayal → Forgive Others
- Solar Plexus = guilt, regret → Forgive Self
- Throat = silencing, shame → Allow Others to Forgive You

Let the **body lead the release**.

Reflection Prompts (Client or Practitioner Use):

"What part of this story still holds the most emotion?"
"If I could say one thing without fear, what would it be?"
"Do I feel ready to release the past—or am I still asking for justice?"
"What step feels the most loving to begin with today?"

Just for today, I will let go of worry and trust the flow of life.

Adjusting Language for Emotional Truth and Breath-Based Release

Letting Forgiveness Flow with Honesty, Gentleness, and Reiki Support

In karmic healing, forgiveness is not always immediate. Clients often arrive carrying lifetimes of pain, betrayal, regret, and unresolved energy. While the goal may be to say "I forgive…"—it's important to remember:

Healing happens when the heart is ready, not when the words are forced.

That's why we adjust the language of forgiveness to match the client's (or our own) current emotional truth. We soften the edges, honor the resistance, and let the **energy move gently—sometimes through breath rather than words.**

The Power of Language in Energy Work

Words carry vibration. They either open the heart… or trigger resistance. In Reiki practice, we aim for **energetic honesty** over spiritual performance.

Use phrases that feel emotionally safe and spiritually aligned. When needed, **guide the client to choose words that reflect their readiness.** The energy will follow.

Step 1: Adjusting Language for Readiness

If a client isn't ready to say "I forgive," offer these softer, truthful alternatives:

Permission-Based Phrases:

"I give myself permission to begin forgiving..."
"I'm willing to explore what it feels like to release this..."
"I may not be ready to fully forgive, but I am ready to stop carrying this pain."
"I allow myself to open just a little... for peace."

These phrases **signal willingness**, which is often the true turning point in a session.

Step 2: Silent Forgiveness + Breath Release

Sometimes, even these words feel like too much. That's when you **let the breath speak**.

Encourage the client to whisper—or even **silently think**:

"I forgive..." (without needing to name the person or story)

Then invite them to:

- Inhale deeply
- Exhale slowly, **with sound** (a sigh, a hum, or even a moan if needed)
- Feel the **emotion leave the body with the breath**

Repeat until the energetic charge softens.

Just for today, I will let go of worry and trust the flow of life.

You might say:

"You don't have to say it out loud. Let your breath be the release. Just feel it move through."

Reiki Support for This Process

As the practitioner:

- Place your hands on the **heart, throat, or solar plexus**
- Let Reiki hold the frequency of **safety and surrender**
- If the client cries, allow it. **Tears are a form of exhale.**
- Say: *"You don't have to do it all today. Even this step is enough."*

Sometimes, the words come after the breath.
Sometimes, the breath is the prayer.

Reflection Prompts:

"What version of the forgiveness phrase feels truest for me right now?"
"What do I feel when I speak or think the word 'forgive'?"
"Can I allow my body to release what my mind still holds onto?"

Emotional Release Cues

How the Body Shows You That Healing Is Happening

When you're working with deep emotional, karmic, or ancestral energy—especially during forgiveness, regression, or Reiki-based clearing—it's important to recognize the **subtle signs that release is occurring.** These cues often don't look dramatic... but they are **evidence that energy is shifting, moving, and leaving the body.**

What Are Emotional Release Cues?

These are involuntary physiological responses that happen as the **nervous system resets**, energy unblocks, and emotional patterns are discharged. They may happen during Reiki, guided visualization, breathwork, or even silence.

Many clients aren't aware that these are **good signs**—they may apologize or try to suppress them. Your job as a practitioner is to **normalize them, honor them, and celebrate them.**

Just for today, I will let go of worry and trust the flow of life.

Common Release Cues (And What They Mean)

Cue	What It Indicates
Crying	Grief, sadness, or long-held emotion is surfacing and being released
Burping	Blocked or stagnant energy is leaving the body, especially from the gut or solar plexus
Yawning	The body is shifting from sympathetic to parasympathetic (relaxation + reset)
Sighing	Emotional tension is releasing; often signifies acceptance or surrender
Stomach sounds	The vagus nerve is activating—sign of nervous system regulation and deep healing
Laughter	A breakthrough has occurred—emotion has transmuted into lightness or joy
Tingling or temperature shifts	Energy movement or chakra activation is underway
Tears without emotion	Ancestral or subconscious release— healing happening at deep levels

These are not side effects. These are success signals.

What to Say to Clients During Release

"That's good—let it move."
"That's just your energy body processing and clearing."
"Whatever wants to come up is safe here."
"Your body knows how to let go. Trust it."

Reinforcing that **nothing is wrong** helps the client **surrender more deeply.**

Practitioner Tip

If a client is holding back emotion, gently say:

"If something's trying to move, you don't need to hold it back. Whatever comes up here is welcome."

Sometimes, simply giving permission **unlocks the release.**

Reflection Prompts (Post-Session or Journal Use):

"What physical or emotional sensations did I notice during the release?"
"Did anything surprise me about how my body responded?"
"Do I feel lighter, clearer, or more grounded afterward?"

Just for today, I will let go of worry and trust the flow of life.

Movement + Voice Activation Techniques

When Energy Won't Release Through Stillness—Use the Body and Voice

While Reiki is often practiced in stillness, some karmic or emotional energy is so deeply embedded that it **requires movement and sound to be fully released.** This is especially true for patterns stored in the root, throat, or solar plexus chakras—where trauma often manifests as stagnation, suppression, or tension.

Movement and voice activation are powerful tools to **loosen stored energy, unfreeze trauma, and re-engage the body's natural processing mechanisms.** These techniques can be used *during* or *after* a Reiki session or as part of a self-guided clearing ritual.

Why Movement Matters

Trauma and suppressed emotion often lodge themselves in the:

- Hips (grief, survival fear)
- Shoulders (burdens, responsibilities)
- Throat (unspoken truth)
- Belly (shame, guilt, ancestral memory)

Movement **wakes up the nervous system** and allows stagnant energy to rise to the surface, where it can be cleared through breath, sound, or Reiki.

Why Voice Activation Works

The throat chakra governs:

- **Expression**
- **Boundaries**
- **Authenticity**
- **Power**

Many clients suppress what they really want to say—or were silenced in the past. Vocalization **reclaims this power**, especially in cases of karmic contracts tied to silence, submission, or fear of speaking the truth.

Simple Movement + Voice Activation Techniques

Toe Wiggling or Foot Stomping

- Reconnects the body to the earth
- Helps release stuck root chakra energy
- Great for post-session grounding

"With each step, I let go. I release, I return, I reclaim."

Walking Meditation (or Slow Pacing)

- Movement while repeating mantras
- Helps integrate forgiveness or soul clarity
- Especially helpful after a past-life regression

Walk slowly while saying:
"I am safe to move forward. My path is clear. My body remembers peace."

Just for today, I will let go of worry and trust the flow of life.

Yelling or Humming Into a Pillow

- Releases emotion safely when verbal expression is blocked
- Soothes the vagus nerve
- Effective for anger, fear, or grief release

Invite the client to:

- Scream into a pillow
- Moan or hum until they feel a shift
- Repeat: *"This is leaving me now."*

Shaking the Body (Gentle or Wild)

- Trauma-informed technique for releasing stored fear
- Especially powerful for ancestral energy
- Let the client shake hands, feet, shoulders, hips—like an animal after stress

Headstands or Legs-Up-the-Wall

- Changes perspective
- Moves stuck energy from the lower chakras upward
- Can release emotional congestion from the heart or gut

Use caution: not for clients with dizziness or high blood pressure.

Bonus: Vocal Toning or Sounding

- Ask the client to hum or vocalize a vowel:

  "Ahhh," "Ohhh," "Eee," "Uuu," or "Mmm"

- Each sound resonates with a chakra
- Let them follow their intuition—no need for perfect pitch

Example: "Ahhhh" for the heart; "Mmm" for grounding.

Reflection Prompts:

"What movement or sound helped me feel more free?"
"Where in my body do I still feel tight or shut down?"
"If I could move or speak one truth without fear, what would it be?"

Just for today, I will let go of worry and trust the flow of life.

How to Muscle Test Completion of an Issue

Using the Body's Innate Wisdom to Confirm Healing Integration

Muscle testing (also known as applied kinesiology) is a powerful tool to **verify whether an issue has been fully released or if residual energy still needs attention.** Since the body doesn't lie, muscle testing allows the **subconscious mind and energy field to answer directly**—bypassing mental doubt, overthinking, or emotional attachment.

This makes it an ideal technique to **check completion after forgiveness work, cord release, past life regression, or ancestral healing.**

Why Use Muscle Testing Here?

- It confirms whether the session has reached **energetic closure**
- It helps the client **trust their own inner knowing**
- It ensures the **root** of the issue has been addressed— not just the surface layer
- It gives you, as a practitioner, a **non-verbal confirmation of release**

Step-by-Step: Basic Self Muscle Testing (Finger Ring Method)

This is a great method for self-check or for clients to use post-session:

1. **Form an O-ring** by connecting the thumb and middle finger of your non-dominant hand.
2. With your dominant hand, use your thumb and index finger to gently try to pull the ring open.
3. Ask a baseline question to calibrate:

   "My name is [your name]." (Should test strong—ring stays closed)
   "My name is [wrong name]." (Should test weak—ring breaks open)

4. Now ask:

   "Has this issue been fully cleared from my energy field?"
   "Is there any remaining emotional charge around this event/pattern?"
   "Do I still hold karmic entanglement with [person/situation]?"

If the ring stays **strong** = completion
If the ring breaks **easily** = further work may be needed

Just for today, I will let go of worry and trust the flow of life.

Alternative: Practitioner Muscle Testing on a Client

Use the **arm test** while the client stands or lies down:

1. Have them hold their arm out parallel to the floor.
2. Apply gentle downward pressure while they **say the test phrase aloud** (e.g., "I am at peace with this," or "This issue is complete.")
3. A **strong** response = truth/integration
4. A **weak** response = unresolved layers or emotions

You can also test for **readiness**:
"Is the client ready to move on to the next layer?"
"Is forgiveness complete at this time?"
"Does this issue require further ancestral/past life work?"

Important Notes:

- Always clear your energy field before muscle testing to avoid biased results.
- Ensure the client is hydrated—**dehydration can block accurate muscle testing.**
- Don't test immediately after emotional overwhelm. Wait for the energy to settle.
- Trust the first answer. Repeating too many times can confuse the energy field.

Reflection Prompts:

"How did it feel to get a 'yes' or 'no' from my body?"
"Do I trust what my energy field is telling me?"
"What will I do next based on this insight?"

How to Handle Client Vulnerability After Release

Supporting Emotional Integration and Creating Safe Space After Deep Healing

After a client experiences a **karmic release, ancestral clearing, past-life regression, or forgiveness breakthrough**, their energy field becomes **wide open**. Emotions may be raw, insights may feel overwhelming, and the client may not yet understand the full significance of what just occurred.

As a practitioner, your role doesn't end with the energy shift—it continues through the **stabilization and integration phase.**

Release is only half the journey. The other half is support, safety, and sacred holding.

Why Clients Feel Vulnerable After Deep Healing

- They've accessed repressed emotions or memories
- Their identity may be shifting ("Who am I without this wound?")
- Energetic cords or patterns they relied on for "security" are gone
- The nervous system is still adjusting
- Their conscious mind is still catching up to the soul-level release

Just for today, I will let go of worry and trust the flow of life.

How to Hold Space Effectively

1. Normalize the Vulnerability

Let them know it's natural to feel raw, tired, emotional, or confused.

"Your energy field is adjusting—this is a beautiful sign that healing occurred."
"Tears, silence, or even emotional numbness are normal. There's nothing wrong with you."
"You don't need to make sense of it all right now. Your body and soul are integrating."

2. Offer Grounding Practices Before They Leave

- Have them stand barefoot for a few minutes
- Offer a drink of water or grounding tea
- Guide a brief breathwork practice or use essential oils (e.g., vetiver, cedarwood, frankincense)
- Suggest they walk or journal before re-entering the outer world

"You've done big work. Give your system space to settle before jumping back into your day."

3. Reinforce Their Strength

Avoid treating them as fragile. Instead, **validate their courage**.

"What you did today takes strength. Most people run from this kind of work."
"You're not broken—you're brave. That emotion moved through you because you're ready."

"This vulnerability is sacred—it means you're no longer hiding from yourself."

4. Provide Optional Integration Support

- A follow-up message the next day
- A journal prompt or reflection sheet
- An optional short meditation or Reiki self-care tip
- Encourage a salt bath, gentle movement, or time in nature

5. Honor Their Privacy

If they shared something intense or personal, **don't reference it casually** in future sessions unless they bring it up first. Let them **choose what to revisit.**

Ethical Note for Practitioners:

Never interpret or define a client's release for them. You may witness something powerful but **don't assign meaning unless invited.** Instead, gently ask:

"How did that feel for you?"
"What do you feel has shifted?"
"Is there anything you need before we close today?"

Let them own their breakthrough.

Just for today, I will let go of worry and trust the flow of life.

Reflection Prompts for Practitioners:

"Did I hold the session with safety, sensitivity, and sovereignty?"
"How can I offer deeper integration without overstepping?"
"What's one thing I can add to my closure practice to make it more nurturing?"

Soul Case Reflection

Lexi's Breaking Point and Breakthrough with Susannah

(Adapted from Journey of a Soul)*

Some karmic patterns cannot be unraveled through reason alone—they must be **felt, broken, and witnessed** at the level of the soul. In this story, we return to Lexi's spiritual path and her pivotal encounter with a soul-bound pattern involving Susannah.

This was not a surface conflict. It was **lifetimes deep.** And it brought Lexi to her emotional edge.

The Breaking Point

Lexi, exhausted and emotionally drained, found herself once again entangled in the energetic signature of **resentment, duty, and silent suffering**—the same pattern that had haunted her in both this life and many others. She was repeating it with Susannah: the cycle of trying to save someone who didn't want to be saved.

No matter how much Reiki, prayer, or wisdom Lexi applied, the knot remained.

Until she broke.

In a moment of raw vulnerability, Lexi fell to her knees—**not in defeat, but in surrender**. She admitted her truth:

Just for today, I will let go of worry and trust the flow of life.

"I don't know how to fix this anymore. I've tried everything. I've given everything. And it still hurts."

It was in that precise moment—when she stopped trying to *earn* her healing and instead **allowed herself to be witnessed by Spirit**—that everything shifted.

The Breakthrough

In the silence that followed her breakdown, Lexi heard the whisper of an ancient voice:

"It is not yours to carry. You never had to fix her. Only to love and release."

With tears streaming down her face, Lexi placed her hands on her own heart, invoked Reiki, and spoke three powerful truths:

1. **"I forgive myself for trying to save someone who chose their own pain."**
2. **"I forgive Susannah for not choosing the light I offered."**
3. **"I allow her to forgive me for walking away—for freeing myself."**

As the words left her lips, a wave of energy moved through her body. She felt it leave her chest, her solar plexus, and her throat. Her breath deepened. Her spine softened. The bond was not "cut"—it was **dissolved at the root.**

Susannah remained in her path, but no longer in her field.

Lesson from the Field

What Lexi experienced was not just the end of a personal conflict—it was the **completion of a karmic loop** that had spun through lifetimes. It was the energetic closing of a contract written in pain and finally released in love.

She did not need Susannah's apology to be free.
She needed only to stop carrying the story.

Reflection Prompts:

"Where in my life have I tried to fix someone else's healing journey?"
"Am I holding on to someone because I feel responsible for their suffering?"
"What would change in my energy field if I allowed them—and myself—to be free?"

Just for today, I will let go of worry and trust the flow of life.

Tool: The I Forgives Worksheet & Journal Page

Release Emotional Weight. Reclaim Your Power. Reset Your Energy Field.

This worksheet is designed to help you—or your client—move through the I **Forgives Method** with honesty, compassion, and energetic precision. It can be used after Reiki sessions, during personal healing rituals, or as part of a forgiveness practice for ancestral, karmic, or relational clearing.

Before You Begin: Create Sacred Space

- Light a candle or incense
- Place your hands over your heart and solar plexus
- Activate Reiki (if attuned)
- Breathe deeply into the body and say aloud:

"I am ready to lighten my spirit. I forgive, not to forget—but to be free."

Step 1: Forgive Yourself

(For mistakes, guilt, shame, survival responses, old patterns)

Write out anything you've been carrying that belongs to **your own self-judgment** or blame.

"I forgive myself for…"
"I allow myself to release…"

"Even though I didn't know better then, I choose to grow now."

How does your body feel after writing this?

Step 2: Forgive Others

(For betrayal, abandonment, silence, harm, or karmic roles)

Write their name(s) or the situation, and let the words rise honestly.

"I forgive _____ for..."
"Even if they never change or apologize, I choose to be free."
"They do not need to carry this burden with me anymore."

What emotion comes up as you write this?

Step 3: Allow Others to Forgive You

(For unspoken harm, walking away, choosing freedom, ending soul contracts)

"I allow _____ to forgive me for..."
"Even if they never do, I send peace to the space between us."
"I call all my energy back to me, whole and healed."

What part of you feels more whole after this?

Just for today, I will let go of worry and trust the flow of life.

Breath & Release

Close your eyes. With every **inhale**, breathe in light.
With every **exhale**, breathe out heaviness.

Optional phrases:

"I breathe in truth. I breathe out pain."
"I breathe in freedom. I breathe out the past."
"I breathe in love. I breathe out the story."

Repeat for 3–5 minutes until your body feels lighter.

Final Affirmation:

"I forgive. I am forgiven. I am free."
"I carry no one's story but my own."
"My energy is mine now—and I choose peace."

Integrating I Forgives for Family Patterns

Ancestral Release Through the Power of Compassionate Awareness

Once you've practiced the *I Forgives Method* on personal experiences, you can begin to extend it beyond yourself— into the energy of your **ancestral line**. This is where karmic healing becomes **multi-generational**, and your inner work ripples through time.

Ancestral healing is not about blame—it's about liberation. It's the courageous act of saying:

"The pain stops with me."

These **forgiveness statements** are designed to help you release unconscious vows, emotional inheritance, and energetic burdens passed down through your lineage—often carried silently, and for far too long.

Use These Practices With Intention:

Before you begin, sit in stillness. Breathe deeply. Activate Reiki.
Place your hands over your heart and solar plexus.
Say softly:

"I now invite healing across all timelines. I am ready to free what no longer belongs to me."

Just for today, I will let go of worry and trust the flow of life.

Ancestral I Forgives Statements:

"I forgive myself for carrying this pattern forward."
"I forgive my ancestors for teaching this pain through silence, survival, or fear."
"I allow them to forgive me for letting go."
"I forgive the lineage for what it did not know, and I bless it with love as I evolve."
"I forgive myself for believing I had to suffer to stay loyal."
"I allow the weight of this pattern to dissolve across time, space, and generations."

Let each phrase **rise gently** from your lips, or write them in your journal.
If tears come, let them. If stillness comes, honor it.
Reiki will carry your words into the memory of your bloodline.

Optional Visualization:

As you speak these affirmations, imagine a long cord running through your family tree—threading through generations behind and ahead of you. See that cord begin to glow, fray, and gently **dissolve in light.** The love remains. The burden does not.

Closing Blessing:

"I heal not only for myself, but for those who came before me—and those who will come after.
May this release bring peace to my ancestors, freedom to my soul, and light to the path of all who follow."

Cross-Link Resource: Watch "Forgiveness Release" on YouTube

Title: *Forgiveness Release*
Watch it here: https://youtu.be/3ZU4RUgpjfc

To support and deepen your healing journey, we've created a companion video to guide you through the **emotional release process using the I Forgives Method**.

In this video, you'll:

- Learn how to begin forgiveness gently and truthfully
- Be guided through a heart-centered release with Reiki energy
- Witness how movement, breath, and intention create a shift
- Be reminded: *you are not alone on your healing journey*

When to Watch:

- After journaling with the *I Forgives Worksheet*
- When you're feeling emotionally blocked or heavy
- To process a past event, relationship, or ancestral wound
- As part of your regular Reiki self-practice or client aftercare

Just for today, I will let go of worry and trust the flow of life.

Suggested Companion Practice:

After watching the video, return to your journal or worksheet and ask:

"What moved in me?"
"What still wants to be seen?"
"What truth surfaced when I let go?"

Forgiveness isn't just a concept—it's a frequency. And sometimes, it helps to be guided into that space. Let the video hold you in that space of safety, release, and renewal.

PART 7:
THE SCIENCE BEHIND
TAPPING TECHNIQUES

Just for today, I will let go of worry and trust the flow of life.

Chapter 7: The Science Behind Tapping Techniques

Why Tapping Works

A Science-Based Look at BodyTalk, EFT & Energetic Rewiring

Tapping techniques like **BodyTalk** and **Emotional Freedom Technique (EFT)** may appear simple on the surface— rhythmic tapping on specific areas of the body—yet they are grounded in powerful physiological, neurological, and energetic principles. These modalities work because they engage the **entire mind-body-energy system** in a way that promotes healing on multiple levels at once.

Here's Why Tapping Works:

1. Activates Brain Processing Centers

Tapping stimulates areas of the brain responsible for **emotional regulation, memory processing, and self-awareness**, including the **prefrontal cortex** (logic and reason) and the **limbic system** (emotion and threat response). When we tap while focusing on a specific issue, it helps the brain safely **reprocess stored trauma or distress** without becoming overwhelmed.

Tapping helps turn the "survival brain" down and the "healing brain" on.

2. Calms the Nervous System & Vagus Nerve

Tapping on areas like the **head, heart, and gut** sends a signal through the **autonomic nervous system**, shifting the body from a sympathetic (fight-flight-freeze) state to a parasympathetic (rest-digest-heal) state. This includes direct stimulation of the **vagus nerve**—the body's longest cranial nerve—linking the brain to the heart, lungs, and digestive tract.

This shift allows healing, insight, and emotional release to occur safely.

3. Accesses and Clears Energetic Disruptions

According to **Traditional Chinese Medicine (TCM)** and modern energy medicine, our life force energy (Qi or Prana) flows through a network of meridians. Emotional and physical trauma can create blockages or stagnation within this flow. Tapping helps to **dislodge and clear these energetic disruptions**, restoring communication between the body's systems and rebalancing the field.

In essence, tapping helps your energy body reboot.

4. Harnesses the Power of Neuroplasticity

By combining **intention, sensation, and emotional awareness**, tapping strengthens new neural pathways and weakens the old ones that reinforce patterns of stress, trauma, or limitation.

Just for today, I will let go of worry and trust the flow of life.

This is neuroplasticity in action—**rewiring the brain and body to respond differently to old triggers.**

Every tap is like pressing a reset button on the body's stress memory.

5. Reinforces Mind-Body-Spirit Integration

Tapping synchronizes **mental clarity, emotional release, physical calm, and spiritual awareness.** It allows the conscious and subconscious minds to communicate, clearing energetic imprints from the body's biofield and rewriting the emotional narrative stored in the cells.

In Summary:

Tapping works because it:

- Activates emotional processing in the brain
- Calms the nervous system and vagus nerve
- Clears meridian-based energy blockages
- Rewires patterns through neuroplasticity
- Bridges the conscious and subconscious for integrated healing

Whether you're using EFT, BodyTalk, or your own intuitive tapping system, the results stem from this elegant fusion of modern science and ancient energy wisdom.

.

BodyTalk Tapping: A System-Wide Healing Reset

Accessing the Body's Innate Intelligence Through Light, Rhythm, and Focus

BodyTalk Tapping is a unique, holistic healing technique that blends **neuroscience, quantum principles, Traditional Chinese Medicine**, and **energy psychology** to restore communication within the body-mind system. Unlike EFT, which focuses primarily on emotional regulation through specific meridian points, BodyTalk works on a broader level—**letting the body's innate intelligence guide the healing process**.

Tapping in BodyTalk is not random. It follows a rhythmic sequence designed to **"wake up"** the body's internal systems and **reestablish energy flow and interconnection**.

How It Works

In BodyTalk, the practitioner identifies energetic or structural imbalances through muscle testing or intuitive scanning. Once the priority area is found, the client (or practitioner) taps gently over the:

- **Head** – to stimulate the brain and initiate rewiring
- **Heart** – to store the changes in the body's electromagnetic field
- **Gut** – to integrate the shift into the subconscious and emotional centers

Just for today, I will let go of worry and trust the flow of life.

Each tap sends a pulse through the **nervous system and meridians**, instructing the body to correct and harmonize itself based on the new priority revealed.

The head represents awareness and neurological response.
The heart records the shift.
The gut processes it on an intuitive and emotional level.

Science Behind BodyTalk Tapping

- **Neuroscience** confirms the brain's ability to form new patterns when attention is combined with physical stimulus (i.e., tapping).
- **Quantum theory** supports the idea that focused intent and energy fields can change matter.
- **The vagus nerve**, activated during heart and gut tapping, supports emotional regulation, immunity, and deep rest.
- **Energy medicine** teaches that rhythms and micro-movements can clear stagnant fields and rebalance systems.

When to Use BodyTalk Tapping

- When the issue feels unclear, buried, or layered
- When a client is overwhelmed and needs calm without conversation
- After energetic release to "lock in" the healing shift
- In combination with Reiki to deepen integration
- As part of ancestral or subconscious pattern clearing

Try It Yourself: Mini BodyTalk Tapping Ritual

1. Focus on a symptom, belief, or emotion you're ready to shift
2. With intention, **tap lightly on the top of your head** while holding the focus
3. Tap gently over your **heart center** with both hands
4. Tap or rest your hand on your **navel** (solar plexus or gut)
5. Breathe and repeat 2–3 times
6. Say silently:

"My body knows what to do. I allow this shift to integrate fully."

You don't need to know exactly what's wrong. Your body does. BodyTalk Tapping simply gives it permission to fix what's been forgotten.

Just for today, I will let go of worry and trust the flow of life.

EFT: Emotional Freedom Technique

Tapping to Release Emotional Blocks and Rewire the Body's Response to Stress

Emotional Freedom Technique (EFT) is a powerful method of self-healing that combines **gentle tapping on acupuncture meridian points** with **focused emotional statements**. Rooted in both **Traditional Chinese Medicine** and modern **psychology**, EFT allows us to acknowledge painful emotions while reprogramming how the mind and body respond to them.

EFT works on the principle that **"the cause of all negative emotion is a disruption in the body's energy system."** By physically tapping on key meridian points while voicing truth-based affirmations, you can **dislodge stuck energy, reduce emotional intensity, and create space for healing.**

The Science of EFT

EFT activates several healing mechanisms at once:

- **Acupressure stimulation** calms the amygdala (your fear center), reducing stress and emotional intensity
- **Repetition of affirmations** rewires cognitive and emotional patterns through **neuroplasticity**
- **Exposure and acceptance** of emotion (naming what you feel while tapping) reduces avoidance and trauma loops
- Studies have shown EFT reduces cortisol levels, anxiety, depression, and even physical pain

You are literally reprogramming your body's reaction to memory, pain, or fear—in real time.

Core Components of EFT

The Setup Statement

This is the phrase you repeat while tapping on the **karate chop point** (side of the hand).

"Even though I feel [emotion or problem], I deeply and completely accept myself."

This creates space for emotional honesty while affirming self-acceptance.

The Sequence

You tap through 8 meridian points while focusing on the issue:

1. Eyebrow
2. Side of the eye
3. Under the eye
4. Under the nose
5. Chin
6. Collarbone
7. Under the arm
8. Top of the head

Repeat the emotion or shortened reminder phrase at each point (e.g., *"this anger," "this fear," "this tension in my chest"*).

Just for today, I will let go of worry and trust the flow of life.

Try It Yourself: EFT in 5 Steps

1. **Identify the issue.** Choose a specific emotion, belief, or memory.
2. **Rate the intensity** (0–10). This gives you a baseline to track change.
3. **Say the setup statement** while tapping the side of your hand:

   "Even though I feel [emotion], I deeply and completely accept myself."

4. **Tap through the eight meridian points**, repeating a reminder phrase (e.g., "this grief," "this tightness in my chest").
5. **Pause. Breathe. Re-rate the intensity.** Repeat if needed.

When to Use EFT:

- When a specific emotion is overwhelming or intrusive
- When you need to **release old beliefs or trauma loops**
- To calm the nervous system before or after a Reiki session
- As a daily practice to **neutralize emotional triggers**

"EFT lets you speak the unspoken, feel the unfelt, and release the energy that has stayed trapped for too long."

Reflection Prompts:

"What emotion is asking to be heard, not fixed?"
"What truth did I avoid that I can now gently name?"
"How did my body feel before, during, and after tapping?"

Just for today, I will let go of worry and trust the flow of life.

Cross-Link Resource: EFT Tapping for Emotional Release

Video Title: *EFT Tapping for Releasing Emotional Blockages*
Watch it here: https://youtu.be/n1lesBOsm7E

To support your journey through forgiveness, karmic healing, or ancestral release, this guided video demonstrates how to use **Emotional Freedom Technique (EFT)** in a clear, accessible way.

In this video, you'll learn:

- How to use the EFT tapping points effectively
- What to say during each phase of emotional release
- How to shift the energy of pain, fear, anger, or grief
- A complete walkthrough of a tapping session for deep healing

When to Use This Video:

- After journaling with your *I Forgives* statements
- When emotions are rising and need to be lovingly released
- Before or after a Reiki or regression session
- Anytime you feel "stuck" and need help moving the energy

Let this video hold space for you while you tap into your truth, feel your emotions fully, and come home to your peace.

Tapping Comparison Chart: BodyTalk vs. EFT vs. Energetic Tapping

Feature / Focus	BodyTalk Tapping	EFT (Emotional Freedom Technique)	General Energy Tapping
Primary Intention	Restore communication and balance throughout body systems	Clear emotional blockages and rewire reactions to trauma or stress	Move stuck energy and emotions gently out of the system
Guiding Intelligence	Body's innate wisdom determines what to heal	Conscious focus on specific emotional issue	Intuition or intention-based flow
Tapping Points	Head, Heart, Gut	Face, upper body, and hand meridian points	Any energy centers, chakras, or intuitive points
Verbal Component	Optional or silent—no verbal	Required—affirmations used during	Optional—can use mantras,

Just for today, I will let go of worry and trust the flow of life.

Feature / Focus	BodyTalk Tapping	EFT (Emotional Freedom Technique)	General Energy Tapping
	affirmations needed	tapping sequence	breath, or silence
Tools Used With	Often used with muscle testing, intuitive scanning, Reiki, or energy protocols	Often combined with talk therapy, affirmations, journaling	Often used with meditation, Reiki, energy healing, or rituals
Emotional Access	Can access subconscious and ancestral patterns without needing full emotional recall	Requires emotional engagement with specific issues for best results	Gentle emotional engagement or intention-based release
Scientific Foundations	Neuroscience, vagus nerve stimulation, quantum healing, TCM	TCM meridians, neuroplasticity, trauma theory, cognitive restructuring	Energetic clearing, vibrational psychology, chakra theory

Feature / Focus	BodyTalk Tapping	EFT (Emotional Freedom Technique)	General Energy Tapping
Practitioner vs. Self-Use	Best guided by trained practitioner for deeper layers	Easily used solo or with a coach/therapist	Often used independently for self-care or in intuitive sessions
Best For	Complex energetic imbalances, ancestral cords, subconscious patterns	Specific emotional issues, phobias, trauma, limiting beliefs	Everyday energetic hygiene, post-session clearing, intention work

Summary:

- **BodyTalk**: System-wide, intuitive, and practitioner-guided
- **EFT**: Structured, emotional, and highly accessible for self-use
- **General Tapping**: Flexible, intuitive, and energetically supportive

Each method works—choose the one that resonates with your current need, intention, or emotional bandwidth. Or blend them to create your own soul-centered practice.

Just for today, I will let go of worry and trust the flow of life.

Optional: Silent Tapping Sequence for Emotional Integration

A BodyTalk-Inspired Script Without Verbal Affirmations

Sometimes, healing doesn't need words—just presence, rhythm, and breath.
This **no-words-needed tapping sequence** is perfect when:

- You're feeling emotionally raw or overwhelmed
- You don't know what to say—but feel something needs to shift
- You've just completed forgiveness work or released deep emotion
- You want to trust your **body's innate intelligence** to do the work

Silent Tapping Sequence

1. **Focus on the feeling**
   Bring your awareness to the area of discomfort, emotion, or tension.
   You don't need to name it. Just be with it.
2. **Begin tapping lightly on the top of your head**
   - Use both hands or one.
   - Tap for 10–20 seconds.
   - Breathe slowly and deeply.
3. **Move your hands to your heart center**
   - Tap gently over the center of your chest.
   - Feel warmth, release, or stillness.
   - Let the body soften.
4. **Tap your navel or lower belly**

- o This integrates the shift into your subconscious and gut instinct.
  - o Imagine grounding or releasing anything that's no longer needed.
5. **Place your hands still over your heart or belly**
   - o Rest and breathe.
   - o Imagine golden light flowing through you.

No words, just rhythm, presence, and trust.

Optional Finishing Statement (Silent or Whispered):

"My body knows how to heal.
My energy is safe to shift.
I am whole. I am light. I am free."

Just for today, I will let go of worry and trust the flow of life.

Integrate the Healing Physically

Once emotional release has occurred through your **I Forgives sequence**, it's important to let the **body catch up with the energy shift**. While the mind may understand that something has changed, the nervous system and energy field still need gentle confirmation. That's where **light tapping** comes in— offering your system a rhythm, a message, and a new pattern to embody.

Tip: Seal the Shift with Tapping

After completing your I Forgives sequence, take a moment to anchor the healing into your energy field.

Use gentle tapping on the following areas:

- **Head** – to reprogram the mind and release mental loops
- **Heart** – to store the emotional shift in your electromagnetic field
- **Gut** – to integrate the change at a subconscious and intuitive level

"Tap, breathe, and affirm: *This healing is complete. I am free.*"

PART 8.
DAILY KARMIC
HEALING PRACTICE

Just for today, I will let go of worry and trust the flow of life.

Chapter 8: Daily Karmic Healing Practice

Daily Karmic Healing Practice
Building a Sacred Practice: Morning & Evening Rituals

Healing karmic and ancestral energy isn't just something we do during big spiritual breakthroughs—it's a **daily act of intention**. By creating a simple, consistent practice, you train your energy field, your nervous system, and your soul to stay clear, aligned, and in harmony with your evolution.

Think of it like brushing your energetic teeth.
Small moments of reflection and release each day prevent the build-up of emotional plaque.

Morning Ritual: Begin in Alignment

Purpose: Set your vibration for the day, consciously choose how you want to show up, and gently dissolve residual karmic energy from dreamtime or the past.

Suggested Practice (5–10 minutes):

1. **Hand on Heart & Belly**
   Take 3 deep breaths. Say silently:

   "I return to myself. I step into today with lightness and sovereignty."

2. **Reiki Self-Treatment (Short Version)**
   Place your hands on your crown, heart, and solar plexus.
   Let Reiki flow. Trust it knows where to go.

3. **Forgiveness Whisper**
   Ask: "Is there anything I'm already holding today?"
   If a memory or person comes to mind, say:

   "I forgive you. I forgive myself. I choose peace."

4. **Tapping Seal (Optional)**
   Tap head, heart, and gut while breathing deeply.

5. **Mantra for the Day**
   Choose one:

   "I am clear. I am grounded. I am guided."
   "I walk today free from old stories."
   "I choose to lead with compassion and truth."

Just for today, I will let go of worry and trust the flow of life.

Evening Ritual: Clear, Reflect, and Close the Loop

Purpose: Release the energy of the day, cut emotional cords, and gently resolve any karmic echoes that arose in thoughts, interactions, or dreams.

Suggested Practice (5–15 minutes):

1. **Stillness or Breathwork**
   Sit or lie down. Breathe slowly into your belly.
   Say silently: *"I call my energy back to me now."*

2. **Review the Day with Compassion**
   Ask: "Where did I give away my energy today?"
   "Where was I reactive or ungrounded?"
   "What needs to be forgiven or released before sleep?"

3. **I Forgives Reflection**
   Speak or journal 1–3 forgiveness statements:

   "I forgive myself for…"
   "I forgive _____ for…"
   "I allow them to forgive me for…"

4. **Reiki Flow or Tapping (Optional)**
   Let Reiki run through your palms into your body for integration.
   Or do a silent head-heart-gut tapping sequence.

5. **Closing Statement or Blessing**

   "I release this day. I call back my power. I rest in peace."

Why These Rituals Matter

Daily karmic clearing doesn't prevent you from ever feeling hurt or stuck again. But it **shortens the time you stay there**, and it keeps the energy body agile, conscious, and resilient. Over time, the layers fall away faster, and your reactions become more aligned with **who you are becoming—not who you've been.**

Small daily acts of release become your soul's declaration: "I am ready to live beyond my past."

Just for today, I will let go of worry and trust the flow of life.

Daily "I Forgives" Reset Practice

Release Yesterday. Reclaim Today. Reset Your Soul.

Each day offers a chance to **begin again**—but many of us carry the weight of yesterday into today without realizing it. Residual emotions, self-judgment, or minor unspoken moments can build up in the energetic body, creating unseen heaviness.

This simple daily *I Forgives Reset* is designed to **clear the slate gently**, so you can realign with peace, clarity, and forward momentum. It takes only a few minutes, yet its ripple effect can change the way your entire day unfolds.

Morning or Evening Practice (2–5 Minutes)

1. **Place one hand on your heart and the other on your solar plexus**
   o Breathe deeply
   o Feel the rise and fall of your body as you center in truth
2. **Speak or Whisper These Phrases Silently**
   (Repeat as needed, or speak them aloud for stronger release)

   "I forgive myself for yesterday."
   "For what I said or didn't say… for what I felt or held back… I forgive myself now."
   "I forgive others for any pain or missteps—intentional or unconscious."
   "I allow others to forgive me, so I can move forward in

peace."

"I carry no residue of regret. I walk in grace."

3. Tapping Seal (Optional)

- o Tap gently on your head, heart, and gut while breathing out the past
- o Affirm: *"I am new. I am clear. I am free."*

Forgiveness doesn't need to be dramatic or deep every time. Sometimes, it's just a quiet agreement with yourself that you won't carry today what was meant to be left behind.

Just for today, I will let go of worry and trust the flow of life.

Spring / Wood Element Daily Karmic Healing Practice

For the Season of Renewal, Growth, and Forgiveness of the Past

Best for: Spring months, Wood Element imbalances, Spring Equinox, liver/gallbladder healing, or new beginnings

Morning Practice – *Awaken with Purpose and Direction*

1. **Stretch & Breathe**
   - Stand tall. Inhale and stretch your arms up like tree branches.
   - Exhale slowly and let your hands fall to your sides.
   - Say: *"I grow with grace. I release the weight of yesterday."*
2. **Reiki to Liver + Solar Plexus**
   - Hands on upper abdomen and right ribcage (Wood element organs)
   - Let Reiki flow to any tension, stagnation, or anger stored there
   - Imagine green light filling your body with vitality
3. **Forgiveness Statement for Spring**

   "I forgive myself for the times I pushed too hard or gave up too soon.
   I now choose flow, flexibility, and trust in my growth."

4. **Tapping Seal**
   - Gentle taps on head, heart, and gut
   - Smile at yourself in the mirror: *"I am growing in the right direction."*

Evening Practice – *Releasing Frustration and Cultivating Clarity*

1. **Evening Reflection**
   Ask:
   - "Where did I feel blocked or frustrated today?"
   - "Where did I compromise my truth to keep peace?"

2. **I Forgives for Control, Anger, and Past Decisions**

   "I forgive myself for needing to control what was never mine."
   "I forgive others for decisions that redirected my path."
   "I allow space for new growth where there was once pain."

3. **Reiki to the Feet (Rooting and Clearing)**
   - Send energy down through your legs
   - Visualize roots anchoring you to Earth's spring renewal

4. **Closing Blessing**

   "As nature blossoms, so do I. I am ready. I am open. I am free."

Just for today, I will let go of worry and trust the flow of life.

Optional Spring Equinox Ritual:

- Write one belief or pattern you're ready to release on paper
- Bury it in soil or plant it under a new seed or flower
- Say: *"I let the Earth transform this. I begin again."*

Summer / Fire Element Daily Karmic Healing Practice

For the Season of Expansion, Joy, and Heart-Centered Alignment

Best for: Summer months, Fire Element imbalances, Summer Solstice, heart and small intestine meridians, or when healing from burnout, overgiving, or heartbreak

Morning Practice – *Ignite the Light Within*

1. **Sunlight Activation**
   - Step outside or face the sun. Place your hands over your heart.
   - Inhale deeply and smile with gratitude.
   - Whisper: *"I receive today with joy. My heart is open."*
2. **Reiki to the Heart & Shoulders**
   - Place hands over your chest and then each shoulder
   - Let Reiki soothe any tension from overgiving, grief, or emotional fatigue
   - Visualize radiant red or golden light spreading through your chest
3. **Seasonal Affirmation**

   "I allow joy to flow through me freely. I lead with love—not fear."
   "My passion is sacred. My light is safe."

4. **Tapping Seal + Laughter Release**

Just for today, I will let go of worry and trust the flow of life.

- o Tap lightly on head, heart, and gut
- o Bonus: Let yourself laugh—even if you fake it at first. Let joy ripple through

Evening Practice – *Cool the Flames, Restore the Spirit*

1. **Cooling Breath or Cold Water Ritual**
   - o Splash cool water on your face or wrists
   - o Exhale heat, tension, or overstimulation from the day
   - o Say: *"I release all that burns unnecessarily. I return to peace."*

2. **I Forgives for Heart-Related Patterns**

   "I forgive myself for abandoning my own joy."
   "I forgive others for breaking my trust."
   "I allow my heart to forgive me for ignoring its whispers."

3. **Reiki for Soul Warmth**
   - o Hands over the heart and solar plexus
   - o Imagine a soft ember glowing in your center—nurtured, not consumed

4. **Closing Blessing**

   "I rest in my radiance. I burn away what is no longer true.
   I choose softness, not sacrifice."

Optional Summer Solstice Ritual:

- Light a candle or bonfire at sunset
- Speak aloud one truth your heart has reclaimed this season
- Say: *"As the light peaks, so does my power. I honor my passion, and I trust its rhythm."*

Just for today, I will let go of worry and trust the flow of life.

Late Summer / Earth Element Daily Karmic Healing Practice

For the Season of Integration, Nourishment, and Centering in the Self

Best for: Late Summer (between seasons), Earth Element imbalances, digestive health, overthinking, caretaking fatigue, codependency, or after major energetic shifts (like healing work, spiritual downloads, or emotional processing)

Morning Practice – *Return to Your Center*

1. **Grounding Body Awareness**
   o Sit or stand with both feet on the ground
   o Place one hand on your belly and one on your heart
   o Say: *"I return to my center. I nourish myself first today."*
2. **Reiki to the Solar Plexus and Spleen**
   o Hands just above the navel and on the left side under ribs
   o Imagine golden-yellow light warming and stabilizing your core
   o Let Reiki dissolve overthinking, worry, and emotional overwhelm
3. **Seasonal Affirmation**

   "I am worthy of care. I am grounded in trust. I am supported by Earth."
   "I give to myself with the same devotion I've given to others."

4. **Tapping Seal + Soft Belly Breaths**
   - Tap gently on the head, heart, and gut
   - Breathe into your belly: *"I am safe. I am centered. I am whole."*

Evening Practice – *Digest, Reflect, and Soothe*

1. **Digestive Reflection**
   Ask:
   - "What emotional energy did I take in today?"
   - "What am I still chewing on that needs to be let go?"

2. **I Forgives for Caretaking and Self-Forgetfulness**

   "I forgive myself for putting others ahead of my own peace."
   "I forgive the parts of me that confuse overgiving with love."
   "I allow myself to receive nourishment without guilt."

3. **Reiki to Digestive Center**
   - Place both hands on the belly
   - Visualize energy spiraling in a slow, grounding circle—clockwise
   - Let Reiki support healthy boundaries and self-containment

4. **Closing Blessing**

   "I am enough. I am held. I am at peace within myself. I digest the day and release what is not mine to keep."

Just for today, I will let go of worry and trust the flow of life.

Optional Ritual for Earth Element or Seasonal Transition:

- Place one smooth stone or bowl of grains in your hand
- Say aloud one thing you're ready to integrate or ground
- Place the item on your altar or in the soil, saying:

"I anchor this truth. I trust the unfolding."

Autumn / Metal Element Daily Karmic Healing Practice

For the Season of Letting Go, Reflection, and Honoring the Sacred Within

Best for: Fall months, Metal Element imbalances, Autumn Equinox, lungs and large intestine meridians, grief, perfectionism, ancestral connection, or emotional clutter

Morning Practice – *Clarity Through Breath and Intention*

1. **Deep Breath with the Season**
   o Stand near an open window or step outdoors
   o Inhale the crisp morning air slowly
   o Exhale with intention: *"I let go. I receive what is mine."*
2. **Reiki to the Lungs and Throat**
   o Place hands on your chest and then over your throat
   o Let the breath guide the Reiki energy in and through the lungs
   o Visualize white or silvery light clearing inner space
3. **Seasonal Affirmation**

   "I release what no longer serves me with gratitude. My truth does not need to be perfect—it only needs to be mine."

Just for today, I will let go of worry and trust the flow of life.

4. **Tapping Seal + Breath Sync**
   - Tap head, heart, and gut while matching the rhythm of your breath
   - Use each tap as a pulse of surrender, grace, and renewal

Evening Practice – *Reflection and Graceful Release*

1. **Letting Go Reflection**
   Ask:
   - "What do I no longer need to carry?"
   - "What am I clinging to out of fear, habit, or identity?"

2. **I Forgives for Grief and Control**

   "I forgive myself for holding on too long."
   "I forgive others for not giving closure I hoped for."
   "I allow myself to grieve without judgment."
   "I give myself permission to begin again."

3. **Reiki to Lower Lungs and Colon Area**
   - Place one hand on your chest and the other just below your navel
   - Visualize stale energy releasing downward with each exhale

4. **Closing Blessing**

   "As the leaves fall, so does my attachment. I release what is done.
   I carry only what is sacred."

Optional Autumn Equinox Ritual:

- Write down old beliefs, identities, or fears on small pieces of paper
- Bury them beneath leaves, or release them in wind or water
- Say: *"As the Earth releases, so do I. I am ready to create space."*

Winter / Water Element Daily Karmic Healing Practice

For the Season of Stillness, Inner Reflection, and Deep Ancestral Listening

Best for: Winter months, Water Element imbalances, approaching or during Winter Solstice (Yin peak)

Morning Practice – *Return to the Depths of You*

1. **Silence + Stillness (2–3 minutes)**
   o Sit with your hands over your lower belly (kidney/water center)
   o Visualize dark, still water—deep, wise, undisturbed
   o Say silently: *"I trust the wisdom that lives in my stillness."*

2. **Reiki Pulse to the Lower Chakras**
   o Focus Reiki on your root and sacral chakras
   o Imagine blue/black light swirling and anchoring your energy

3. **Seasonal Mantra**

   "Even in silence, I am growing. I honor my stillness as sacred."

4. **Tapping Seal (Optional)**
   o Gentle taps on head, heart, and gut
   o Breathe into your back—feel support from within

Evening Practice – *Release and Reflect in the Waters of the Soul*

1. **Water Element Invocation**
   - Light a candle or sit by water (bath, bowl, sound)
   - Whisper: *"I release all that is not mine to carry."*
2. **I Forgives for Lineage and Fear**

   "I forgive myself for fearing my own power."
   "I forgive the silence passed through my bloodline."
   "I allow my ancestors to forgive me for stepping into light."

3. **Reiki for Ancestral Healing**
   - Place your hands on your sacral and heart chakras
   - Visualize your ancestors behind you in soft blue light
4. **Closing Blessing**

   "I honor the unseen. I release the weight. I return to the depth of peace."

Optional Winter Solstice Ritual:

- Write down all the emotional weights you've carried this year
- Burn or bury them on Solstice night
- Say: *"I descend into the darkness to be reborn in light."*

Just for today, I will let go of worry and trust the flow of life.

MODULE 9:
THE ROLE OF THE REIKI
PRACTITIONER IN
KARMIC HEALING

Chapter 9: The Role of the Reiki Practitioner in Karmic Healing

The Role of the Practitioner — Guide, Not Guru

Stepping into the role of a **Reiki Karmic Healing Practitioner** is both a privilege and a responsibility. You're not just holding space for healing; you're helping clients **navigate the energetic residue of lifetimes**, ancestral burdens, and soul-level patterns. This work goes beyond technique—it calls for **compassionate presence, energetic neutrality, and spiritual humility.**

The most important thing to remember?

You are a guide—not a guru.

Why This Distinction Matters

- **A guide** helps others find their way by offering tools, safety, and support.
- **A guru**, in contrast, places themselves as the ultimate source of truth or authority.

Just for today, I will let go of worry and trust the flow of life.

In karmic healing work, the practitioner must **never create dependence**, claim superiority, or speak over the client's intuitive truth. Instead, we meet the client as an **equal soul on the path**—one who may simply be walking a few steps ahead in a particular domain.

The Practitioner's Role Includes:

Holding Safe Energetic Space

You create a calm, grounded, non-judgmental container where the client's nervous system can soften and their higher self can speak. You are **not fixing them—you are witnessing their unfolding**.

Asking Questions, Not Giving All the Answers

Your job is to help them access their inner knowing—not to project yours.
Instead of saying: *"This is your karmic issue,"* ask:

"What does this pattern feel like it connects to?"
"Where have you felt this before?"
"What truth is trying to surface beneath this pain?"

Staying Energetically Clean

Do your own clearing before and after sessions. Clients may unconsciously place you in a "healer" or "rescuer" role—**don't accept the projection**. Stay grounded, humble, and connected to Reiki, not ego.

Empowering the Client

Always leave the client with a tool, ritual, or reflection to continue the work on their own. Healing continues after the session ends.

"Your client should leave feeling empowered, not dependent."

What You Are:

- A channel for Reiki and truth
- A witness to the soul's remembering
- A mirror for the client's strength
- A co-creator of sacred healing space

What You Are Not:

- A psychic authority on someone's karma
- A savior or energetic cleaner for others
- The source of their healing—you are a facilitator, not the force

Reflection Prompts (For Practitioners):

- "Am I guiding this session from ego or intuition?"
- "Do I feel the need to impress, fix, or prove something?"
- "How can I remind the client of their own power today?"
- "What are my energetic boundaries when holding space for karmic work?"

Just for today, I will let go of worry and trust the flow of life.

Reiki Ethics in Karmic Work

Holding Integrity in Deep Spiritual and Emotional Healing

When working with karmic energy, ancestral wounds, or past life themes, the **ethical responsibility of the Reiki practitioner deepens.** You're no longer just moving energy—you're entering sacred, often subconscious territory that may carry deep emotion, trauma, and spiritual contracts.

This is where your role as a **clear, compassionate, and grounded facilitator** becomes essential. Ethical practice ensures that the **client's sovereignty remains intact**, the session stays safe, and healing unfolds at a pace the soul can truly integrate.

1. Emotional Boundaries: Holding, Not Absorbing

Karmic sessions can bring intense emotional releases—grief, rage, fear, even past-life memories. It's natural to feel compassion, but **it is not your role to carry the client's pain.**

What to do instead:

- Be present. Breathe. Hold the energy without merging with it.
- If emotions arise in you, ground yourself through your feet and Reiki flow.
- After the session, **clear your field** and thank the energy for moving through—not into—you.

"You are a container, not a sponge."

2. Honoring the Client's Soul Path

As insights, visions, or intuitions arise, remember:

The client's path is their own. You are not here to dictate it.

Avoid statements like:

- "This is what your karma is."
- "You were this in a past life, and you must now fix it."
- "If you don't forgive them now, you'll carry it forever."

Ethical reframes:

- "What do you feel this energy wants to show you?"
- "Does that memory feel symbolic or emotionally true for you?"
- "Would you like to explore releasing that together, or does it need more time?"

Always offer choices and avoid prescriptive or absolute declarations. Even if you see or sense something intuitively, **never override the client's inner wisdom.**

3. Staying Grounded During Sessions

Grounding is your anchor, especially when clients go into deep karmic layers or emotional regression. If you are not grounded, you may:

- Lose track of time
- Merge with the client's energy
- Feel drained, dizzy, or overwhelmed afterward

Just for today, I will let go of worry and trust the flow of life.

Daily grounding practices for karmic work:

- Eat something warming and earthy before and after sessions
- Tap or rub the bottoms of your feet
- Use grounding stones (e.g., hematite, black tourmaline, smoky quartz)
- Visualize roots anchoring you to the Earth before every session
- Close each session with the statement: *"I am clear. They are clear. We are each whole."*

Grounding protects you. Boundaries protect the work.

Reflection Prompts (Practitioner Ethics Check-In):

- *"Am I holding space or stepping into their healing for them?"*
- *"Am I speaking from ego or offering guidance from neutrality?"*
- *"Is the energy still with me after the session? If so, what do I need to release?"*
- *"Did I empower the client to own their healing experience?"*

Session Structure for Reiki Karmic Healing

A Flow for Safe, Soul-Level Transformation

A well-structured session offers both **freedom and focus**—giving space for intuition while also creating a grounded, safe container for the client's healing journey.

Below is a recommended structure for a **Reiki Karmic Healing session**, whether you're focusing on past life regression, ancestral patterns, or emotional cord release. It balances deep energetic work with practical aftercare.

1. Intake Interview (10–15 Minutes)

Purpose: Establish trust, gather relevant history, and identify the client's emotional or karmic focus.

Ask:

- "What recurring emotion, thought, or situation do you feel stuck in?"
- "Has this shown up in other relationships or life stages?"
- "Do you feel this may be connected to something deeper—ancestral or past life?"

Let the client speak freely. Listen not just for words, but **for energetic patterns or emotional cues**.

Just for today, I will let go of worry and trust the flow of life.

Tip: Avoid leading questions—let their language guide the work.

2. Regression or Pattern Discovery (Optional – 10–20 Minutes)

Purpose: Gently access the root layer—whether past life, ancestral, or early life imprinting.

Choose one of the following approaches based on client readiness:

- **Guided Regression Visualization** (e.g., "Train Ride" method)
- **Timeline Tracking** ("When did this emotion first begin?")
- **Symbol or Body-Based Insight** ("Where do you feel this in the body? What does it remind you of?")

Invite the client to explore what surfaces without overanalyzing. Encourage emotional truth, not literal accuracy.

You are opening the memory field—not proving anything.

3. Reiki + I Forgives Application (20–30 Minutes)

Purpose: Begin energetic clearing while applying forgiveness language and healing intention.

Steps:

- Begin Reiki, focusing on relevant chakras (heart, solar plexus, sacral, throat)

- Gently introduce "I Forgives" phrases if appropriate (spoken by you or the client)
- Allow silence, emotion, or intuitive imagery to unfold naturally

Examples:

"I forgive myself for carrying this pain across lifetimes."
"I forgive my ancestors for their silence."
"I allow _____ to forgive me so we may both be free."

Incorporate light **tapping**, **breathwork**, or **chakra visualization** as needed.

4. Energy Clearing & Integration (5–10 Minutes)

Purpose: Seal and stabilize the energetic shift.

- Use Reiki symbols or intuitive hand placements to **clear lingering residue**
- Visualize golden light or soft color washing through the aura
- Tap lightly on the head, heart, and gut to seal the session (optional)
- Invite the client to imagine cords dissolving or karmic threads untangling

Final statement to guide closure:

"Your energy is now clear. You are free to move forward lighter, wiser, and whole."

Just for today, I will let go of worry and trust the flow of life.

5. Post-Session Guidance (5–10 Minutes)

Purpose: Support emotional integration and empower the client after the session ends.

Offer:

- A journaling prompt (e.g., "What truth did I reclaim today?")
- A simple self-Reiki or grounding practice
- A personalized affirmation or I Forgives phrase
- Reminders that **emotions may surface over the next 1–3 days**

Optional follow-up:

- Suggest a check-in session in 1–2 weeks
- Share a link to your *Forgiveness Release* or *Regression* YouTube videos

Your role now shifts from practitioner to witness. Let the client own their healing.

Using Muscle Testing to Track Progress

Letting the Body Speak the Truth Beyond Words

In karmic Reiki healing, the conscious mind doesn't always know when something has fully shifted—but the **body always knows**. That's where **muscle testing** (also known as applied kinesiology) becomes an invaluable tool. It allows you to **track energetic changes, uncover hidden blocks**, and verify if the healing work is complete or if another layer remains.

Whether used during intake, mid-session, or follow-up care, muscle testing helps both the practitioner and the client move forward with confidence.

Why Use Muscle Testing in Karmic Healing?

- Confirms if a karmic pattern has been released or needs further attention
- Reveals subconscious resistance to healing or forgiveness
- Helps determine which part of a process to focus on next
- Offers **energetic validation** of the client's intuitive shifts
- Encourages **client self-trust** through body-based answers

The energy field never lies. Muscle testing lets the body speak when the mind is unsure.

Just for today, I will let go of worry and trust the flow of life.

Basic Testing Methods

For Practitioners (on Clients):

Use the **Arm Test**:

1. Have the client extend one arm parallel to the floor.
2. Ask a **yes/no statement** while applying gentle pressure to the wrist or forearm.
3. A **strong response** = truth or energetic alignment
4. A **weak response** = emotional charge, blockage, or untruth

Example statements:

- "This karmic pattern has been cleared."
- "There is more to release before integration is complete."
- "This client is ready to move forward without this pattern."

For Self-Use or Client Homework:

Use the **Finger Ring Method**:

1. Connect the thumb and middle finger on the non-dominant hand (creating a ring).
2. Interlock with the thumb and index finger of the other hand, forming a second ring.
3. Try to break the ring while saying a test phrase:
    - "My name is [correct name]" (strong)
    - "My name is [incorrect name]" (weak)

Then test relevant phrases like:

- "I have fully forgiven myself for this."
- "This emotion is still stored in my energy field."
- "I am ready to release this belief/pattern completely."

When to Use Muscle Testing in a Session

- **Before regression** → to confirm which issue or lifetime is ready to be addressed
- **During I Forgives work** → to determine if more layers need clearing
- **After energy clearing** → to verify if the field is clear and integrated
- **During follow-up** → to track healing progress and readiness for deeper layers

Let the client's own energy set the pace. The muscle response keeps the work safe and precise.

Ethical Reminder:

Always test from a **neutral, grounded state**. Clear your own field beforehand.
Muscle testing is a **conversation with the energy field**, not a diagnostic tool or psychic reading.

Reflection for Practitioners:

- "Am I using testing to empower or control?"
- "Do I honor what the test reveals, even if it surprises me?"
- "Am I grounded and neutral when testing this client?"

Just for today, I will let go of worry and trust the flow of life.

How to Tell if the Client Is Done or Needs More Work

Reading the Subtle Signs of Completion in Karmic Healing

In Reiki karmic healing, knowing when to **complete the session or continue deeper** is a subtle art. While some sessions naturally reach a point of clarity and release, others may still carry unresolved energy—even when the client feels emotionally "done."

As a practitioner, your job is not to rush, force, or prolong the healing—but to **attune to the signs of integration vs. the signals of unfinished work.**

Signs the Client Is Complete for Now: These cues suggest the healing has reached a **safe stopping point**—even if more work may unfold in the future:

Energetic Indicators:

- Breathing slows and deepens
- The body visibly relaxes (muscles release, face softens)
- Chakra flow feels balanced or unobstructed
- The aura feels smooth, grounded, or "sealed"

Emotional/Spiritual Indicators:

- The client expresses **clarity**, peace, or a sense of closure
- They no longer feel emotionally "charged" about the original issue

- Insight arises naturally (e.g., "I understand now," or "I feel free")
- A spontaneous release occurs (crying, laughing, sighing, yawning)

Testing Confirmation:

- **Muscle testing** affirms statements like:

  "This issue has been cleared."
  "No further release is needed today."
  "The client is in a state of integration."

Signs the Client May Need More Work:

These cues suggest that **energetic or emotional residue** still lingers and may need to be addressed in this or a future session:

Energetic Indicators:

- The energy field feels "sticky" or overly heavy
- Certain chakras still feel blocked, closed, or overactive
- Heat, tightness, or pulsing remains in one area of the body

Emotional/Spiritual Indicators:

- The client still feels agitated, anxious, or numb
- They struggle to express what shifted (or say nothing has)
- New memories or emotions surface late in the session

Just for today, I will let go of worry and trust the flow of life.

- They say: "I feel like something's still there," or "I can't let go of it yet"

Testing Confirmation:

- Muscle testing reveals a weak response to:

  "I am clear of this pattern."
  "I have completed this emotional release."
  "This karmic energy is fully resolved."

What to Do If More Work Is Needed

- **Honor the limit** of the current session—don't force a breakthrough
- Acknowledge the layer that surfaced and suggest:

  "This was one important layer. Would you be open to exploring the next one in another session?"

- Offer **home practices**: journaling, daily I Forgives, tapping, grounding rituals
- Let the client know **integration is part of healing,** and more may unfold naturally

Healing is not a race. It's a rhythm. Trust the tempo of the soul.

Practitioner Reflection:

- "Am I trying to finish for them, or am I letting the energy speak?"
- "Does the client feel empowered or dependent on 'more work'?"

Follow-Up Practices and Reinforcement

Supporting Integration After the Session Ends

Healing doesn't stop when the client leaves your treatment space—in many ways, it **begins** there. Karmic Reiki work stirs energy at the root: emotional, ancestral, and soul-level patterns. As these unravel, the client may experience **physical symptoms, emotional shifts, vivid dreams, or new insights** in the days that follow.

Your role as a practitioner includes **equipping them with gentle follow-up tools** that reinforce the release, ground their energy, and support continued transformation—without dependence on you.

1. Self-Reiki or Reiki-Infused Meditation (5–10 Minutes Daily)

Encourage the client to:

- Place hands over their **heart, solar plexus**, or any area of release
- Breathe and say silently: *"I integrate this healing with grace."*
- Visualize soft light flowing through their body

If they aren't Reiki attuned, suggest they:

- Use **breath and intention** to bring calm energy to their body
- Listen to a **Reiki-infused meditation** or healing music

Just for today, I will let go of worry and trust the flow of life.

2. I Forgives Journal Prompting

Offer them a few **daily forgiveness statements** to explore in their own words. For example:

"Today, I forgive myself for…"
"I allow others to forgive me for…"
"I release this pattern of…"

Encourage gentle honesty—**no judgment, no pressure to be profound.**

3. Grounding Rituals (Especially for Sensitive Clients)

Healing from karmic work can open the energy field. Offer practical grounding tools:

- Walk barefoot on earth (weather permitting)
- Use grounding essential oils: vetiver, patchouli, cedarwood
- Carry stones like smoky quartz, black tourmaline, or red jasper
- Take an Epsom salt bath within 48 hours to release energetic residue

4. Gentle Movement & Breathwork

Stored emotions may continue to surface. Suggest:

- Stretching, yoga, Qi Gong, or shaking out the limbs
- Breathing into the lower belly while saying:

    "I feel safe in my body. I am present. I am whole."

5. Integration Window: 1–3 Days

Let the client know it's normal to feel:

- Emotionally tender or sensitive
- Physically tired or lighter
- Spiritually open or dreamy

Encourage them to **rest more, hydrate well**, and avoid over-stimulating environments if possible.

"Trust what comes up after the session. The body is integrating truth."

6. Optional Practices You Can Provide as a Practitioner:

- A short **"Integration Reiki Recording"** for them to use at home
- A **custom journaling sheet** based on their session's theme
- A **Tapping Practice Handout** (silent or emotional release script)
- A link to your YouTube videos (e.g., *Forgiveness Release, Regression*, etc.)
- An email follow-up within 48 hours to check in and offer continued support

Reflection for Practitioners
"What can I offer that supports their empowerment—not attachment?"
"Did I leave them feeling capable of carrying the healing forward?"
"Have I reinforced their ownership of the process?"

Just for today, I will let go of worry and trust the flow of life.

Teaching Clients Self-Healing Between Sessions

Empowering Continued Growth Outside the Treatment Room

One of the greatest gifts you can offer your clients is **not just a breakthrough in session—but the tools to sustain it afterward.** Karmic healing often unfolds in layers, and between sessions, clients may face emotional echoes, energetic shifts, or a return of old habits.

By teaching **simple, grounded, self-healing practices**, you empower clients to become **active participants in their own transformation**. This reduces dependence on you and strengthens their spiritual confidence and energetic resilience.

Why Self-Healing Matters in Karmic Work:

- It helps **stabilize emotional shifts** and energetic releases
- Encourages **sovereignty** instead of practitioner attachment
- Builds **self-trust** and awareness of personal energy patterns
- Keeps momentum between sessions, preventing regression
- Deepens the integration of forgiveness, regression, and Reiki-based work

Foundational Self-Healing Practices to Teach

1. The Daily "I Forgives" Reset

Encourage clients to speak or write:

"I forgive myself for…"
"I forgive others for…"
"I allow others to forgive me…"

Just a few lines each day can continue to **clear emotional buildup** and **reinforce karmic release.**

2. Head-Heart-Gut Tapping Sequence

Teach them a simple silent tapping ritual:

- **Head** – to clear looping thoughts
- **Heart** – to anchor emotional truth
- **Gut** – to integrate and release into the subconscious

Use after triggers, dreams, or anytime they feel "stuck."

3. Reiki Self-Treatment (if Attuned)

For Reiki-trained clients:

- Emphasize daily self-Reiki to **maintain energetic hygiene**
- Focus especially on heart, solar plexus, and sacral chakras
- Suggest they create a *"sacred moment"* rather than a routine

Just for today, I will let go of worry and trust the flow of life.

For non-attuned clients:

- Offer a visualization: golden light flowing through the palms
- Encourage intentional breath and intuitive hand placement

4. Energy Hygiene Rituals

Teach them to:

- **Brush down the aura** after public interactions
- Use a **salt bath** or **essential oils** after emotional release
- **Visualize releasing cords or inherited patterns** into the earth

5. Anchor in Journaling or Dream Tracking

Prompt clients to record:

- Patterns they notice
- Emotional charges that arise
- Recurring dreams or past-life themes
- Forgiveness insights or resistance points

This encourages **self-reflection without obsession**.

How to Teach It Gently and Effectively

- Introduce one practice at a time—avoid overwhelm
- Frame it as *"support between sessions,"* not "homework"
- Provide handouts or short demo videos when possible
- Check in during follow-ups:

"How did that practice feel?"
"Did anything shift when you used it?"

Your goal isn't to give them a toolbox—it's to help them become the builder of their own peace.

Reflection for Practitioners:

"What practice has helped me the most in my own integration?"
"How can I model empowered healing without needing to fix?"
"Am I guiding them toward sovereignty—or toward returning?"

Just for today, I will let go of worry and trust the flow of life.

MODULE 10:
FROM SOUL MEMORY TO SOUL MISSION

Chapter 10: From Soul Memory to Soul Mission

From Soul Memory to Soul Mission

Uncovering Your Soul's Wisdom Through Regression

Karmic healing isn't just about clearing what holds us back—it's about **remembering who we truly are**. Every lifetime your soul has lived carries not only pain and patterns, but also **gifts, lessons, and wisdom** waiting to be retrieved. Through Reiki-supported regression, we don't just look for trauma—we look for truth.

When clients begin to access their soul memory, they often receive glimpses of their **greater purpose**, calling, or inner archetype. This is the bridge from **past-life imprint** to **present-life mission**.

The Role of Regression in Awakening Soul Purpose

Soul regression (whether spontaneous or guided) allows clients to:

- Access unresolved karmic experiences
- Retrieve **skills, vows, and roles** once held in other lifetimes

Just for today, I will let go of worry and trust the flow of life.

- Recognize recurring soul themes (e.g., teacher, healer, protector, seeker)
- Reconnect with **soul-level strengths** that may have been forgotten
- Understand why they feel drawn to certain people, places, or paths

The memory is not the goal. The wisdom is.

How to Support Clients in Uncovering Soul Wisdom:

1. Ask Reflective Questions After Regression:

- "What do you think your soul wanted you to see in that life?"
- "What quality did that version of you carry that's useful now?"
- "How does that life's ending shape your current view of fear or purpose?"

2. Help Them Translate Memory into Mission:

- "What were you doing in that life that you miss?"
- "Is there a skill, calling, or message that feels familiar now?"
- "What would it look like to bring that version of you into today's life?"

3. Use Reiki to Anchor the Insight:

After the client shares a key realization, offer 1–3 minutes of Reiki with the affirmation:

"I now integrate this wisdom into my present path."

Let the energy body receive what the mind has just remembered.

Common Soul Archetypes That Emerge:

Clients may begin to identify with one or more of the following:

- **The Healer** – drawn to hands-on healing, herbs, or energy work
- **The Teacher** – natural mentor or wisdom-sharer
- **The Seeker** – always exploring spirituality, truth, or knowledge
- **The Guardian** – deeply loyal, protective, or mission-driven
- **The Mystic** – intuitive, visionary, or connected to unseen realms
- **The Builder** – legacy-focused, grounding dreams into reality

Encourage clients not to lock themselves into labels, but to notice what qualities **resonate and reawaken.**

Affirmation for Soul Integration:

"I remember who I am.
I honor where I've been.
I carry the wisdom of lifetimes into the light of this one."

Just for today, I will let go of worry and trust the flow of life.

Practitioner Note:

As a facilitator, stay humble and curious. Don't declare someone's purpose—help them **uncover it through their own felt sense and knowing.**

Regression is not for re-living the past—it's for reclaiming the power it holds.

Aligning with Your Gift Among the Nine Spiritual Gifts

Discovering and Embodying the Spiritual Frequency You Were Meant to Share

As we heal karmic patterns and reconnect with soul memory, many clients begin to ask a deeper question:

"What is my spiritual gift—and how do I live it?"

The Nine Spiritual Gifts, referenced in 1 Corinthians 12:4–11, are not reserved for the chosen few. They are **archetypal energies embedded in all of us**, waiting to be activated as we release fear, trauma, and karmic residue. Each person carries **one or more dominant gifts**, often shaped through the soul's many lifetimes.

In karmic Reiki work, uncovering one's **gift path** is not just about self-knowledge—it's about **soul alignment**.

The Nine Spiritual Gifts: A Brief Overview

1. **The Word of Wisdom** – deep intuitive knowing beyond logic
2. **The Word of Knowledge** – receiving divine insight or guidance
3. **Faith** – a soul-anchored certainty that moves energy and belief
4. **Gifts of Healing** – channeling energy to restore wholeness

Just for today, I will let go of worry and trust the flow of life.

5. **Working of Miracles** – shifting reality through divine force
6. **Prophecy** – speaking truth from higher planes
7. **Discerning of Spirits** – sensing unseen energies or intentions
8. **Different Kinds of Tongues** – channeling energy through spiritual language
9. **Interpretation of Tongues** – decoding or translating spiritual frequency

How to Recognize a Client's (or Your Own) Gift Activation

Watch for these signs during or after a karmic healing session:

- Emotional resonance when hearing about one of the gifts
- Sudden insight or clarity around a long-standing "pull" or purpose
- Past-life memories of using the gift in sacred, mystical, or healing settings
- Recurrent dreams, visions, or synchronicities tied to spiritual service
- An intuitive "yes" in the body when a particular gift is spoken aloud

Questions to Help Clients Align With Their Gift:

- "What do you feel called to share or express that feels *beyond logic*?"
- "Have you ever known something you couldn't explain?"
- "Which spiritual role feels familiar or magnetic—like home?"

- "What do others come to you for—even without knowing why?"
- "Which gift do you feel unworthy of... yet drawn toward?"

Encourage curiosity over certainty—**the gift often reveals itself layer by layer**.

Living in Alignment with Your Gift

Once a client becomes aware of their spiritual gift, invite them to:

- **Dedicate daily time** to connecting with that gift through Reiki, journaling, or meditation
- Use the gift to **serve others gently**, in ways that feel authentic and non-performative
- Notice when ego tries to "control" the gift—return to trust
- Let the gift evolve with them (it may express differently over time)

"You don't need to master your gift. You need only to trust it."

Soul Integration Statement:

"I open to the divine gift within me.
I release all fear of being seen.
I let Spirit express through me, as me, with love."

Just for today, I will let go of worry and trust the flow of life.

Practitioner Reflection:

- "Am I recognizing the sacred in my clients—or trying to define it?"
- "Do I give space for their gift to emerge in its own time?"
- "What is my primary spiritual gift—and how am I living it?"

Using Past Life Lessons to Strengthen Present Power

Transforming Memory into Mastery Through Karmic Insight

Regression work isn't just about healing old wounds—it's about **harvesting wisdom**. Every past life offers a spiritual breadcrumb trail that can lead you back to your core strength. When we revisit these experiences through Reiki-supported karmic healing, we gain access to **deep lessons, dormant gifts, and unclaimed confidence** that are waiting to be integrated into this lifetime.

Rather than reliving pain, we shift the focus to **reclaiming power**—power lost through fear, silence, sacrifice, or trauma.

Why Past Life Lessons Matter in the Present

Past life memories hold:

- **Evidence of resilience** ("I've survived this before.")
- **Unfinished mastery** (gifts or roles that were never fully expressed)
- **Soul contracts** that can now be completed or rewritten
- **Repeating dynamics** that reveal your current growth edge
- **Inner archetypes** that remind you who you truly are

When we learn to recognize the **lesson behind the memory**, it becomes a source of strength—not suffering.

Just for today, I will let go of worry and trust the flow of life.

Karma isn't a punishment—it's a pattern. And pattern offers power when understood.

Questions to Guide the Shift from Lesson to Strength:

After a regression or karmic release session, ask the client:

- "What wisdom did this version of you hold?"
- "What would that past self want you to remember now?"
- "What power did they never get to claim that you can carry forward?"
- "How did they survive, serve, or love in a way that inspires you?"

Help them see that **the strength didn't die with that life—it lives within them now.**

Practical Ways to Anchor Past Life Strength in the Present

1. Reiki Activation Ritual

- While doing self-Reiki (or with a client), focus on a chakra that resonates with the past-life theme (e.g., throat for silenced truth, heart for lost love)
- Say silently or aloud:

   "I reclaim the strength I held in that life. I integrate it into this one."

2. Create a Soul Anchor Symbol

Have the client choose a symbol, color, or word that represents the gift or wisdom they retrieved.
They can:

- Draw it
- Wear it
- Meditate on it
- Use it as a reminder when fear or doubt resurfaces

3. Rewrite the Ending (if needed)

If the past life ended in trauma, failure, or suppression, offer this empowering practice:

- Ask the client to imagine what *should* have happened
- Invite them to rewrite the ending in a way that affirms their power
- Use Reiki to **seal this new energetic imprint**

The body remembers trauma. But the soul remembers truth.
Let the new truth become the stronger voice.

Affirmation for Power Integration:
"I am the living proof of my soul's growth.
I carry the strength of lifetimes.
I walk forward—clear, wise, and whole."

Practitioner Insight:

- "Am I helping the client release the pain but **keep the power**?"
- "Am I asking the right questions to help them extract meaning from memory?"
- "Do I encourage integration—not just recall?"

How to Sense When Your Soul Mission Is Calling

Tuning into the Whisper Beneath the Wound, the Pull Beneath the Pattern

Your soul doesn't shout—it **whispers, nudges, and stirs**. Often, it speaks not in grand visions, but through quiet discomfort, magnetic attraction, or a growing sense that *"there must be more than this."* In karmic healing work, we begin to dissolve the static—ancestral noise, emotional residue, limiting beliefs—so that the **pure signal of your soul mission** can come through.

It's not always a clear message at first. But there are **undeniable signs** that your soul is trying to get your attention.

Signs Your Soul Mission Is Calling

1. Restlessness Without Obvious Cause

You've done the inner work. Life looks "fine" on the outside. But inside, something feels incomplete—like an inner fire is smoldering beneath the surface.

2. Recurring Themes or "Accidental" Signs

You keep encountering the same symbols, professions, spiritual gifts, or historical time periods. These are **breadcrumbs from your higher self.**

Just for today, I will let go of worry and trust the flow of life.

3. Deep Emotional Reactions to Certain Ideas or Images

Whether it's tears, chills, or a racing heart, pay attention to **what moves you without explanation**—especially spiritual, humanitarian, or creative themes.

4. The Old Life Begins to Feel Too Small

Jobs, relationships, or habits that once satisfied now feel restrictive or draining. Your soul is ready to expand beyond the karmic patterns that once defined you.

5. A Pull Toward Service, Expression, or Visibility

You may feel called to teach, heal, create, write, speak, or lead—even if fear still surrounds the idea. The **desire is part of the calling.**

Your mission is often hidden inside what you fear the most… and what you long for the deepest.

Questions to Ask When You Sense the Call

- "What part of me am I no longer willing to silence?"
- "If I stopped being afraid, what would I do?"
- "What do I feel born to contribute—even if I don't feel 'ready' yet?"
- "What keeps finding me—no matter how often I try to ignore it?"
- "What soul work would I do, even if no one applauded?"

Ritual to Strengthen the Signal

1. Sit in stillness. Place one hand on your **heart**, the other on your **solar plexus**.
2. Ask silently: *"What is trying to awaken in me?"*
3. Let images, sensations, or words arise. Don't chase— just receive.
4. Draw or write what came through. It may not make full sense yet—*that's okay.*
5. Offer Reiki to the message with this statement:

   "I allow my soul mission to become known to me, gently and clearly."

Affirmation for Soul Mission Activation:

"I am ready to hear the call.
I trust what is awakening in me.
I allow my life to become a vessel for what I came here to do."

Practitioner Tip:

When your client begins to sense their soul mission:

- Don't define it for them—**ask questions that help them remember**
- Invite them to notice what makes them feel *most alive, most honest, and most whole*
- Remind them: *Purpose is not a job. It's an energy. And it's already inside them.*

Just for today, I will let go of worry and trust the flow of life.

Working with Archangels, Ascended Masters & Spirit Guides

Spiritual Allies in Karmic Healing and Soul Remembrance

In deep karmic and soul-level healing, you are never working alone. Whether consciously invoked or subtly felt, **divine allies—Archangels, Ascended Masters, and Spirit Guides— often appear** to support, guide, and uplift both practitioner and client throughout the process.

These beings exist on higher vibrational planes and can be accessed through **intention, prayer, meditation, Reiki, and energetic attunement.** They are not here to interfere with free will, but to assist in restoring soul alignment, clearing karmic residue, and illuminating your next step.

Why Work With Spiritual Allies in Karmic Healing?

- To **amplify Reiki** energy and bring multidimensional support
- To **receive clarity** when intuitive insight is blocked or clouded
- To **protect and cleanse** the energetic space before and after sessions
- To **offer messages, symbols, or healing frequencies** that transcend language
- To **hold the energetic container** during regression, soul retrieval, or ancestral release

These allies do not do the work for you—but they hold your light while you remember how.

Archangels and Their Healing Roles

Divine Allies in Soul and Karmic Healing

- **Archangel Michael** – Protection, cord removal, strength, clearing fear
- **Archangel Raphael** – Physical healing, emotional soothing, energy integration
- **Archangel Gabriel** – Communication, truth-telling, birth of purpose
- **Archangel Uriel** – Wisdom, illumination of karmic lessons, soul guidance
- **Archangel Zadkiel** – Forgiveness, transmutation of karmic patterns, mercy
- **Archangel Chamuel** – Heart healing, divine love, restoring self-worth
- **Archangel Pistis Sophia** – Spiritual awakening, divine truth, integration of all gifts
- **Archangel Raziel** – Sacred knowledge, soul memory activation, intuitive mastery
- **Archangel Hamied** – Miracles, divine timing, manifestation through higher faith
- **Archangel Bath Kol** – Prophetic insight, divine voice, intuitive communication

Call on them through prayer or inner request—then feel, listen, trust.

Just for today, I will let go of worry and trust the flow of life.

Ascended Masters as Guides of Soul Wisdom

Ascended Masters are souls who have completed the cycle of earthly reincarnation and now serve from higher dimensions.

- **Jesus / Yeshua** – Love, forgiveness, Christ consciousness
- **Kuan Yin** – Compassion, divine feminine grace, mercy
- **St. Germain** – Violet flame, transmutation, karmic cleansing
- **Buddha** – Detachment from suffering, balance, peace
- **Mary Magdalene** – Sacred truth, soul remembrance, divine feminine strength
- **Thoth / Hermes** – Past life wisdom, spiritual knowledge, soul codes

Invite them into sessions where you or your client are exploring **soul contracts, past-life wounds, or karmic soul work**. They often show up symbolically—in colors, phrases, emotions, or inner visions.

Spirit Guides and Personal Soul Companions

Spirit Guides are uniquely assigned to your soul—some from birth, others from past lives or soul contracts. They may appear as:

- Ancestors
- Animal totems
- Light beings
- Energetic presences with specific roles (e.g., gatekeepers, teachers, protectors)

Your client may not "see" their guides, but they may feel:

- Sudden comfort or clarity
- Presence in the room
- Words or images that come unexpectedly
- Emotions that feel *not theirs*, but loving and wise

Help your client learn to **trust what they sense**, even if it isn't visual.

How to Work With These Allies in Session

- **Before the session:** Invite your guides and the client's highest aligned beings into the space

  "I call in the guides, angels, and divine beings aligned with our highest healing. May only love, truth, and light enter here."

- **During the session:** Ask inwardly for support, insight, or energetic reinforcement

  "Show me what this soul is ready to release or reclaim."

- **After the session:** Offer gratitude and dismiss the support gently

  "Thank you for your presence and service. You may now return to your realm."

Affirmation for Sacred Connection:
"I open my energy field only to divine beings of love and light.

Just for today, I will let go of worry and trust the flow of life.

I welcome the allies who walk with me across lifetimes.
I receive their wisdom with grace. I am never alone."

Practitioner Note:
Working with spiritual allies **does not override the client's free will**. Always ask:

- "Is this guidance for me, or for them?"
- "Does sharing this insight empower, or does it create dependency?"
- "Am I interpreting the message clearly—or through my own filters?"

Spiritual allies guide—not dictate. Let them illuminate, not control.

Creating a Soul-Aligned Life

Healing Isn't the End Goal—Living in Alignment Is.

Karmic healing opens the door—but it's how we live afterward that anchors true transformation. Once we begin releasing past life burdens, ancestral loops, and emotional residue, we are no longer driven by unconscious survival patterns. We are free to build a life that reflects our **soul's truth**, not just our inherited wounds.

Living a **soul-aligned life** means making choices in every area—**health, relationships, finances, and purpose**—that resonate with your inner knowing, not outer conditioning.

Health: Listening to the Body as a Spiritual Messenger

When aligned with your soul:

- You nourish your body with food, movement, and rest from a place of reverence—not punishment or control
- Illness and fatigue are treated as invitations to pause and listen—not weaknesses to be ignored
- You understand that healing isn't linear, and your body holds karmic memories too

Ask yourself: "What does my body need to feel safe enough to thrive?"

Just for today, I will let go of worry and trust the flow of life.

Soul-Aligned Practice:

- Use Reiki daily on the solar plexus and root chakra for grounding and vitality
- Speak lovingly to your body before sleep or meals
- Track symptoms or energetic patterns that arise after major emotional releases

Relationships: Rewriting the Karmic Contract

When soul-aligned:

- You no longer stay in relationships from fear, guilt, or obligation
- You recognize karmic mirroring and ask: *"What is this trying to show me?"*
- You choose connections based on resonance, mutual growth, and inner peace—not karmic debt or wounded attraction

You don't need to "fix" people to be worthy of love. You need to be honest about who aligns with your evolution.

Soul-Aligned Practice:

- Use "I Forgives" to clear emotional residue from past or current relationships
- Cut or dissolve cords (with compassion) when a dynamic has completed
- Call in new relationships through heart-based intention, not fear-based need

Finances: Healing the Energy of Worth and Flow

In a soul-aligned life:

- Money becomes a **tool of expression and freedom**, not shame or struggle
- You no longer inherit your ancestors' fear of survival or scarcity
- You view abundance as spiritual alignment, not greed

True wealth is not accumulation—it's trust in your capacity to receive and give in balance.

Soul-Aligned Practice:

- Use Reiki on the root and sacral chakras to clear survival imprints
- Forgive ancestral beliefs around poverty, overwork, or self-sacrifice
- Speak wealth affirmations aligned with service, joy, and integrity

Purpose: Becoming Who You Already Are

When you are aligned with your soul:

- Purpose is not a role—it's a **frequency you live in**
- You follow your intuitive "yes," even when it challenges your comfort zone
- You express your gifts not for validation, but as a natural extension of who you are

Just for today, I will let go of worry and trust the flow of life.

Your soul mission is not something you find—it's something you remember, piece by piece, as you heal.

Soul-Aligned Practice:

- Ask daily: "What does my soul want to create, contribute, or explore today?"
- Journal or meditate on past-life gifts or recurring soul themes
- Create before you consume—live as the source, not the seeker

Integration Ritual: The Soul-Aligned Life Invocation

Place hands over your heart and sacral chakra. Breathe deeply.

Say aloud or silently:

"I release the patterns that no longer reflect my truth.
I forgive the past, and I am open to the present.
May my health, my love, my abundance, and my path reflect the wisdom of my soul.
I choose to live in alignment with who I came here to be."

Case Reflection:

Lexi's Soul Contract and Reincarnation Across Lifetimes

From Karmic Burden to Soul Freedom — A Story from Journey of a Soul

Lexi's journey, as chronicled in *Journey of a Soul*, offers a profound example of how **soul contracts, reincarnation, and karmic healing** intertwine across multiple lifetimes. Her story reflects the very essence of what Reiki Karmic Healing aims to uncover: the unseen threads that bind us to pain, love, and purpose—and the choice to finally break free.

The Repeating Pattern

Throughout her incarnations, Lexi carried a deep soul contract linked to:

- **Abandonment and betrayal in love**
- A spiritual mission that was repeatedly interrupted or silenced
- A powerful karmic bond with Redington—one that crossed timelines, identities, and dimensions

In lifetime after lifetime, Lexi felt called to service, healing, and spiritual truth—but each time, her path was marked by **sacrifice**. She often gave up love for purpose… or purpose for love. The tension between them created **inner conflict and emotional fragmentation** that followed her soul like a shadow.

Just for today, I will let go of worry and trust the flow of life.

The Soul Contract Unveiled

Lexi's karmic entanglement with Redington stemmed from a soul agreement:

They would find each other in every lifetime—but the lesson wasn't a reunion. It was a release.

Through regression, vision work, and spiritual awakening, Lexi began to remember:

- A vow made in a temple long ago to always find him again
- A past life where she sacrificed her mission to save him
- Another where he betrayed her out of fear, repeating the cycle of loss

The pattern was not punishment—it was an invitation to **reclaim herself**.

Breaking the Contract Through Forgiveness and Choice

In her final remembered life, Lexi **chose to forgive him**—not for what he did, but for what the contract no longer served. She said the words:

"I release you. I release the vow. I choose love without suffering."

This moment was not just a healing of one life, but of **many lifetimes.** It allowed her to:

- Stop defining herself by her wounds
- End the soul loop that tied love to sacrifice

- Realign with her true mission as a spiritual teacher and healer
- Open the door to love *that was free, not fated*

Integration Across Lifetimes

In a poetic full-circle, Redington returned—not as the same man, but as a **walk-in soul** in a new body, free of karma. This illustrated one of the highest outcomes of karmic healing:

When the contract is cleared, the soul is free to choose again.

Lexi was no longer bound by vows, suffering, or spiritual servitude. She had moved from karmic repetition to **conscious co-creation.**

Practitioner Insight:

Lexi's story reminds us:

- Soul contracts are real—but they are not prisons. They are **lessons**.
- We must distinguish **love from loyalty**, and **calling from karma**.
- When the soul remembers, **the energy shifts**—and the lifetime changes.

Reflection Prompt for Clients:

"What pattern keeps repeating in your life?
If you could speak to your soul across time, what would you say to set it free?"

Just for today, I will let go of worry and trust the flow of life.

Ritual: Writing Your Soul's Intention Letter

A Sacred Practice to Declare Your Healing, Purpose, and Freedom Across Lifetimes

After karmic release, past life insight, or deep soul remembrance, one of the most powerful next steps is to **consciously declare your new path**. A *Soul's Intention Letter* is not a goal list or affirmation script—it's a sacred written agreement between **you and your higher self**, infused with Reiki, forgiveness, truth, and choice.

Writing this letter signals to your subconscious, your energy field, and the universe:

"I am ready to live from alignment, not from fear. I choose to lead with love, wisdom, and remembrance."

When to Use This Ritual:

- After clearing a karmic pattern or completing a soul contract
- After past life regression or ancestral healing
- At the end of a Reiki Karmic Healing series or program
- During a solstice, equinox, or birthday (rebirth moment)
- When stepping into a new phase of purpose or embodiment

Ritual Steps

1. Prepare Your Sacred Space

- Light a candle or incense
- Place a grounding stone nearby (e.g., hematite, obsidian, smoky quartz)
- Have Reiki flowing or place your hands in Gassho for a few breaths
- Call in your higher self, guides, or Archangels to witness the writing

Optional Opening Affirmation:
"I now write from my highest knowing. May these words reflect the wisdom of my soul."

2. Begin Your Letter with Reverence

You may start with:

"Dear Soul," or
"To the part of me that has walked through lifetimes..."

Then, allow the letter to unfold freely. You might include:

- What you are now choosing to release
- What soul lessons you've learned
- What you forgive (yourself or others)
- What qualities you are ready to embody (e.g., truth, power, peace)
- The way you now choose to live, love, and lead
- A message to your future self—or from your higher self

Just for today, I will let go of worry and trust the flow of life.

3. Seal the Letter with Intention

Close with a vow or declaration:

"From this moment forward, I walk in soul alignment."
"I carry my soul's wisdom with grace and strength."
"I am the author of my life, the keeper of my light, the healer of my line."

Date and sign it with your full name.

4. Energetically Activate the Letter

Hold the letter between your palms and send Reiki to it. Visualize the energy of your intention, infusing every word.

You may say aloud:

"This letter is witnessed by my soul, my guides, and the Universe.
It is done. It is anchored. It is received."

What to Do with the Letter

- Place it on your altar or under a crystal
- Fold it and keep it in a sacred journal or box
- Burn it under the full moon for release and rebirth
- Re-read it whenever you feel lost or disconnected from your purpose

This letter becomes a touchstone. It is your voice—across time, lifetimes, and timelines.

Integration Idea:

For practitioners or group settings, offer this as a closing ritual in:

- Karmic healing circles
- Reiki Master attunements
- Soul purpose retreats
- Past life integration workshops

Just for today, I will let go of worry and trust the flow of life.

Tool: Soul Mission Mapping Worksheet

From Karmic Clearing to Soul Calling — A Visual Guide to Purpose

As clients move through karmic healing, regression, and forgiveness work, a new energy begins to emerge: **clarity.** Often, this clarity isn't about a specific career or title but about a **soul-aligned way of being**—an inner compass that reveals what they're here to embody, express, and contribute.

The **Soul Mission Mapping Worksheet** helps clients visually explore and integrate the insights gained throughout their journey. It is not about finding a job—it's about **mapping the energy of their mission** so it can be expressed in all areas of life.

Purpose of This Tool

- Help clients connect past life lessons to present strengths
- Identify core soul values and patterns
- Clarify how their spiritual gift(s) are meant to serve
- Create an action-aligned vision rooted in truth—not trauma
- Reframe purpose as a *frequency to live*, not a role to chase

Sections of the Worksheet

You can use this as a printable page, a journal prompt, or a client session tool.

1. Past Life Wisdom

What gifts or strengths have appeared in past lives (or deep inner memory)?

- Example: "Healing with hands," "Speaking truth," "Guiding others," "Living in solitude," "Protecting the innocent"

2. Karmic Patterns Released

What major themes or burdens have been healed or released?

- Example: "Self-sacrifice for love," "Fear of speaking," "Witch wound," "Martyr energy"

3. Core Soul Values (This Lifetime)

What matters most to your soul now?
Check or write your own:

- ☐ Freedom
- ☐ Truth
- ☐ Peace
- ☐ Creation
- ☐ Love
- ☐ Teaching

Just for today, I will let go of worry and trust the flow of life.

- □ Justice
- □ Joy
- □ Connection
- □ Wisdom

4. Your Primary Spiritual Gift

Which of the Nine Spiritual Gifts resonates most deeply right now?

- Example: Prophecy, Healing, Faith, Discerning Spirits, etc.
  How might this show up in your daily life or service?

5. Current Mission Theme (In One Sentence)

Write your Soul's current mission in a way that resonates with you:

"To help others remember who they are through..."
"To embody peace in everything I do and say."
"To restore the light in broken places."

6. Next Steps in Embodying This Mission

What aligned action(s) can you take in the next 30 days?

- Example: Launch a healing circle, share my story, begin daily self-Reiki, write a soul blog, say yes to an opportunity, set better boundaries

Final Affirmation:

"My life is an expression of my soul's truth.
Every step I take from here reflects who I came here to be."

Practitioner Tips:

- Use this worksheet at the **end of a multi-session healing journey**
- Offer it as a **post-regression integration tool**
- Create a **guided Soul Mapping session** using this structure
- Pair with journaling, visualization, or an *Intention Letter* ceremony

Glossary

This glossary provides a quick reference for key terms, concepts, symbols, and techniques used in Reiki practice, including details from all three levels of Reiki (Shoden, Okuden, and Shinpiden). It serves as a comprehensive guide to help you deepen your understanding and apply Reiki principles effectively, particularly when working with joints and energy pathways.

A

Alignment – The balanced flow of energy through the chakras, meridians, and nadis. Proper alignment supports emotional, physical, and spiritual health.

Ajna Chakra – The Third Eye Chakra, located between the eyebrows. Governs intuition, perception, and insight.

Anahata Chakra – The Heart Chakra, located in the center of the chest. Governs love, compassion, and emotional balance.

Attunement – A sacred process in which a Reiki Master transfers the ability to channel Reiki energy to a student. Attunements are given during Reiki Level 1, 2, and 3 training.

Auric Field (Aura) – The energetic field surrounding the body. It consists of multiple layers connected to the chakras and reflects emotional, mental, physical, and spiritual health.

Just for today, I will let go of worry and trust the flow of life.

B

Balance – A state where energy flows freely through the body without blockage or resistance. Reiki helps restore balance at the physical, emotional, and spiritual levels.

Breathwork – Techniques that use conscious breathing to direct and enhance the flow of energy through the body.

C

Chakra – Spinning energy centers located along the central axis of the body. There are seven primary chakras and numerous secondary chakras located in the joints and extremities.

Cho Ku Rei – The Power Symbol. Used to increase the flow of Reiki energy, clear blockages, and activate protection.

- Meaning: "Place the power of the universe here."
- Application: Increases power, activates energy flow, and grounds the practitioner.

Cleansing – The process of releasing stagnant or blocked energy from the body or energetic field through Reiki or other energetic practices.

Conscious Intention – Focusing mental and spiritual energy on a specific outcome or goal during a Reiki session.

Crossroad (Energetic) – A point where multiple energy pathways (chakras, meridians, nadis) intersect. Joints often serve as energetic crossroads.

Crown Chakra (Sahasrara) – The seventh chakra, located at the top of the head. Governs spiritual connection and enlightenment.

D

Dai Ko Myo – The Master Symbol. Used in Reiki Level 3 for spiritual awakening, enlightenment, and deeper healing.

- Meaning: "The Great Shining Light."
- Application: Used to heal the soul and promote spiritual growth.

Distance Healing – Sending Reiki energy to a person, situation, or event across time and space using the symbol Hon Sha Ze Sho Nen.

E

Emotional Blockage – Stored emotional trauma or resistance that restricts the flow of energy through the chakras, nadis, or meridians.

Energy Field – The subtle energetic body surrounding and penetrating the physical body.

Energy Knot – A blockage in the flow of energy through a joint, chakra, or meridian.

F

Flow – The smooth movement of energy through the body's energy channels. Reiki restores flow when energy becomes stagnant.

Just for today, I will let go of worry and trust the flow of life.

Flexibility – The ability to adapt emotionally and spiritually, reflected physically in joint mobility.

H

Hand Positions – Specific placements of the hands on or above the body used to channel Reiki energy.

Heart Chakra – See **Anahata Chakra**

Hon Sha Ze Sho Nen – The Distance Symbol. Used to send Reiki across time and space.

- Meaning: "No past, no present, no future."
- Application: Used for healing events in the past, present, and future; also used for distance healing.

I

Ida Nadi – The left energy channel connected to feminine, cooling, and intuitive energy. Ida is linked to emotional balance and the parasympathetic nervous system.

Intuitive Reiki – Allowing Reiki to flow based on inner guidance rather than strict hand placements.

J

Joint – A physical and energetic intersection where multiple meridians and nadis meet. Joints store emotional patterns and influence energy flow throughout the body.

K

Ki – Life force energy that flows through the body's meridians and nadis. Reiki channels this energy for healing and balance.

Kundalini – Spiritual energy coiled at the base of the spine. When awakened, it rises through the chakras, leading to enlightenment.

L

Level 1 (Shoden) – The beginner level of Reiki where students learn:

- The history of Reiki.
- Basic hand positions for self-healing and healing others.
- The concept of ki (life force energy).

Level 2 (Okuden) – The practitioner level where students learn:

- Advanced hand positions.
- Emotional and mental healing.
- Reiki symbols (Cho Ku Rei, Sei He Ki, Hon Sha Ze Sho Nen).

Level 3 (Shinpiden) – The Master level where students learn:

- How to perform attunements.
- Spiritual healing and awakening.
- Master symbol (Dai Ko Myo).

Just for today, I will let go of worry and trust the flow of life.

M

Meridians – Pathways through which qi (life force energy) flows in the body. Used in Traditional Chinese Medicine and Reiki for energy balancing.

Mind-Body Connection – The relationship between emotional, mental, and physical health. Reiki works on all three levels simultaneously.

N

Nadi – Subtle energy channels through which prana (life force energy) flows. There are thousands of nadis, but the three primary nadis are Ida, Pingala, and Sushumna.

O

Okuden – See **Level 2**

P

Pingala Nadi – The right energy channel connected to masculine, heating, and active energy. Pingala is linked to physical energy and the sympathetic nervous system.

Prana – The life force energy that sustains all living beings.

R

Reiki – A Japanese healing technique that channels life force energy through the practitioner's hands into the recipient's body.

- Meaning: "Universal life force energy."

Root Chakra (Muladhara) – The first chakra, located at the base of the spine. Governs security, grounding, and survival.

S

Sahasrara – See **Crown Chakra**

Sei He Ki – The Emotional Symbol. Used to balance emotional and mental energy.

- Meaning: "God and man become one."
- Application: Used for emotional healing and removing mental patterns.

Shoden – See **Level 1**

Shinpiden – See **Level 3**

Solar Plexus Chakra (Manipura) – The third chakra, located at the upper abdomen. Governs confidence, personal power, and digestion.

Sushumna Nadi – The central energy channel that runs through the spine. When open, it allows spiritual awakening and the rise of kundalini energy.

T

Third Eye Chakra (Ajna) – See **Ajna Chakra**

Tsubo Points – Pressure points along the meridians that serve as access points for energy flow. Similar to secondary chakras.

Just for today, I will let go of worry and trust the flow of life.

U

Universal Energy – The source of Reiki energy, believed to be the creative force of the universe.

W

Wisdom Channel – Sushumna Nadi is often called the Wisdom Channel because it governs spiritual awareness and higher consciousness.

REI (ray)

Universal Life Energy
Spiritual Consciousness
All-Knowing

KI (kee)

Breath
Life Force
Vital Radiant Energy

Chokurei (Show Ku Ray)

Used for Physical Clearing.

Forward 7 is used for general or whole body, backward 7 is used for specific or small areas

Sei He Ki (Say Hey Key)

Used for Emotional Clearing and Mental Clearing

Hon Sha Ze Sho Nen, which is specifically associated with distant healing.

Just for today, I will let go of worry and trust the flow of life.

Companion Books

More is taught about Energy healing, Chakras, and Reiki in my book,

"Secrets of a Healer – Magic of Reiki (Vol X)

Trade paperback ISBN: 978-1-7772220-0-0

eBook ISBN 978-1-7772220-1-7

Just for today, I will let go of worry and trust the flow of life.

SECRETS OF A HEALER
VOL. XI
THE REIKI MASTER'S MANUAL

Trade paperback ISBN: 978-1-990062-34-6

eBook ISBN 978-1-990062-35-3

BY DR. CONSTANCE SANTEGO
GRAND REIKI MASTER

Angelic Lifestyle A Vibrant Lifestyle from a Grand Reiki Master

Trade paperback ISBN: 978-0-9952112-7-8

Just for today, I will let go of worry and trust the flow of life.

Angelic Lifestyle 42-Day Energy Cleanse

Trade paperback ISBN: 978-1-7770818-3-6
eBook ISBN 978-1-7770818-4-3

Reiki and the Power of The Joint Points

VOL. I OF THE REIKI WISDOM SERIES

Beyond the Symbols — The Path to True Mastery

Trade paperback ISBN: 978-1-990062-57-5

eBook ISBN 978-1-990062-58-2

Just for today, I will let go of worry and trust the flow of life.

from my "Novel" Series,
"The Nine Spiritual Gifts Granted By Spirit"
Vol IV in the series, *"Miracles of a Soul"*

Soft Cover ISBN: 978-1-990062-12-4
eBook ISBN: 978-1-990062-13-1

Zen Coloring VOL II: Reiki Energy Journal

Therapeutic Art for Mind, Body, and Spirit

Soft Cover ISBN: 979-8324392697

Just for today, I will let go of worry and trust the flow of life.

Bibliography

The following sources include foundational texts on Reiki, Traditional Chinese Medicine, the Five Elements, energy healing, and the emotional-energetic connections within the body. This bibliography reflects a blend of classical Eastern wisdom, modern holistic practices, and practical healing guides. Together, these works provide a well-rounded and deeply rooted understanding of the elemental philosophy and energetic principles explored throughout *Reiki and the Five Elements: Balancing Energy Through Nature's Wisdom*.

Ando, Teruko. *The Art of Reiki: Healing with Universal Life Force Energy*. Tokyo: Ki Publications, 2012.

Beinfield, Harriet, and Korngold, Efrem. *Between Heaven and Earth: A Guide to Chinese Medicine*. New York: Ballantine Books, 1991.

Brennan, Barbara Ann. *Hands of Light: A Guide to Healing Through the Human Energy Field*. New York: Bantam, 1987.

Chopra, Deepak. *The Book of Secrets: Unlocking the Hidden Dimensions of Your Life*. New York: Harmony Books, 2004.

Gerber, Richard. *Vibrational Medicine: The #1 Handbook of Subtle-Energy Therapies*. Rochester, VT: Bear & Company, 2001.

Honervogt, Tanmaya. *The Power of Reiki: An Ancient Hands-On Healing Technique*. London: Hodder & Stoughton, 2000.

Kaptchuk, Ted J. *The Web That Has No Weaver: Understanding Chinese Medicine*. Chicago: Contemporary Books, 2000.

Miles, Pamela. *Reiki: A Comprehensive Guide*. New York: TarcherPerigee, 2006.

Santego, Constance. *Secrets of a Healer: Magic of Reiki*. Kelowna: Maximillian Enterprises, 2022.

Weil, Andrew. *Spontaneous Healing*. New York: Ballantine Books, 1995.

Zhi Gang Sha, Dr. *Soul Mind Body Medicine: A Complete Soul Healing System for Optimum Health and Vitality*. San Francisco: New World Library, 2006.

Note: Additional inspiration and knowledge for this book have been drawn from decades of hands-on practice, student case studies, and the oral teachings passed through the lineage of Reiki Masters and natural healing traditions.

Suggested Internet Resources

These online platforms offer valuable insights into Reiki, the Five Elements, holistic healing, emotional release, and the energetic systems of the body. They provide a mix of educational materials, practitioner tools, scientific research, spiritual guidance, and community support that complement the principles explored in *Reiki and the Five Elements: Balancing Energy Through Nature's Wisdom*. Whether you're seeking meditations, training, or inspiration, these trusted resources can guide you.

Reiki and Energy Healing

- **International Center for Reiki Training** – www.reiki.org
  One of the most comprehensive Reiki hubs, offering training programs, articles, and practitioner directories.
- **Reiki Rays** – www.reikirays.com
  A global Reiki community featuring techniques, hand positions, meditations, and practitioner insights.
- **Reiki Healing Association** – www.reikihealingassociation.com
  Membership-based organization with downloadable tools, certification support, and Reiki business tips.
- **The Reiki Alliance** – www.reikialliance.com
  Founded by students of Hawayo Takata, this site explores lineage, tradition, and global Reiki connection.

Just for today, I will let go of worry and trust the flow of life.

Elemental Wisdom, TCM & Chakra Systems

- **Sacred Centers (Anodea Judith)** –
  www.sacredcenters.com
  Extensive chakra training and books by a leading
  expert in energy psychology and body systems.
- **Chi Nei Tsang Institute** – www.chineitsang.com
  Focus on meridians, chi flow, and internal organ
  energy work from a Taoist healing perspective.
- **The Shift Network** – www.theshiftnetwork.com
  Offers holistic courses and summits on chakra
  balancing, seasonal energy healing, and intuition.

Emotional & Spiritual Healing

- **Louise Hay's Official Website** – www.louisehay.com
  Emotional affirmations, metaphysical insights, and
  mind-body healing techniques.
- **HeartMath Institute** – www.heartmath.org
  Science-backed tools for emotional coherence, stress
  relief, and energetic alignment.
- **EFT Tapping (EmoFree)** – www.emofree.com
  Learn the Emotional Freedom Technique to release
  stored emotional patterns through acupressure.
- **Dr. Joe Dispenza** – www.drjoedispenza.com
  Research and training on consciousness, energy
  medicine, brain states, and quantum healing.
- **Bessel van der Kolk** – www.besselvanderkolk.com
  Pioneer in trauma research and body-based healing.
  Author of *The Body Keeps the Score*.

Sound Healing, Breathwork & Visualization

- **Insight Timer** – www.insighttimer.com
  A free meditation app with Reiki-specific sessions, breathwork, and guided visualizations.
- **Sonic Bloom** – www.sonicbloom.com
  Sound healing resources, frequency charts, and vibrational therapy tools.
- **The Tuning Fork Shop** – www.tuningforkshop.com
  Sound tools for chakra and meridian balancing, including weighted forks and training.
- **Breathwork Alliance** – www.breathworkalliance.com
  A collective of breathwork professionals offering techniques for clearing energy blocks.

Books, Learning Platforms & Media

- **Goodreads** – www.goodreads.com
  Discover book lists, reviews, and reader favorites in energy healing, Reiki, and TCM.
- **Gaia** – www.gaia.com
  Spiritual documentaries, interviews, and courses on vibrational medicine and consciousness.
- **Coursera** – www.coursera.org
  University-level courses in mindfulness, TCM, and holistic health.
- **Open Path Collective** – www.openpathcollective.org
  Affordable access to integrative therapy, energy medicine practitioners, and online healing support.

Just for today, I will let go of worry and trust the flow of life.

Professional Reiki & Holistic Health Organizations

- **International Association of Reiki Professionals (IARP)** – www.iarp.org
  Networking, marketing tools, and global practitioner directories.
- **National Certification Board for Therapeutic Massage & Bodywork (NCBTMB)** – www.ncbtmb.org
  Continuing education provider for Reiki, bodyworkers, and holistic health professionals.
- **Holistic Health Practitioner Network** – www.holistichealthpractitioners.org
  Directory and resource hub for certified energy healers and alternative practitioners.

These online resources can support you in creating a Reiki practice that is **grounded, inspired, and aligned** with the elemental wisdom of nature. May they serve as companions on your ongoing healing journey.

Suggested Video Resources

Films & Documentaries on Energy, Emotion & Elemental Harmony

These video resources expand on the themes explored in this book—energy medicine, elemental balance, emotional patterns, and spiritual growth. Each film or documentary offers insight into the interconnected nature of the body, mind, and spirit. Whether you're a Reiki practitioner, energy healer, or seeker of deeper truths, these titles will inspire and awaken new levels of understanding.

Energy Healing & Vibrational Medicine

The Living Matrix (2009)
Explores the science behind energy healing, consciousness, and quantum biology. Features pioneers in holistic health and the human energy field.

E-Motion (2014)
Reveals how trapped emotions influence physical health and how releasing emotional energy can restore wellness. Perfect companion for elemental emotional healing.

Heal (2017)
A powerful documentary that investigates the connection between mindset, beliefs, and the body's ability to heal. Interviews with leading experts in energy medicine and psychology.

Frequency of Genius (2020)
Explores how sound, frequency, and vibration shape human

Just for today, I will let go of worry and trust the flow of life.

consciousness, health, and transformation. A great link to elemental sound healing practices.

Elemental Wisdom & Nature-Based Healing

Inner Worlds, Outer Worlds (2012)
A spiritual documentary exploring the sacred geometry, vibration, and consciousness that connect all life—bridging the microcosm and macrocosm, much like the Five Elements.

Fantastic Fungi (2019)
While focused on fungi, this film offers deep insight into Earth's natural intelligence, cycles, and the energetic symbiosis of life—wonderful inspiration for Earth element practices.

The Secret Life of Plants (1979)
A classic exploring the emotional and energetic sensitivity of plants—demonstrating energy flow and intuitive connection in the natural world.

Mind-Body-Spirit Connection

What the Bleep Do We Know!? (2004)
A metaphysical journey through quantum physics, consciousness, and the power of belief to reshape our reality. Offers a foundational perspective for Reiki and energetic work.

The Power of the Heart (2014)
Explores how the heart is more than a physical organ—it's a source of intuition, healing, and energetic guidance. Deeply relevant to the Fire element and heart-based Reiki sessions.

You Can Heal Your Life (2007)
Based on Louise Hay's teachings, this film bridges affirmations, energy patterns, and healing. A visual guide to emotional clearing and spiritual self-awareness.

Spiritual Growth, Stillness & Inner Wisdom

The Shift (2009, featuring Dr. Wayne Dyer)
Explores the transition from ambition to meaning, aligning perfectly with the Metal and Water elements' call to let go and listen inwardly.

Awake: The Life of Yogananda (2014)
Follows the life of Paramahansa Yogananda, a pioneer in bringing meditation and energy practices to the West. Inspires spiritual devotion and disciplined energy flow.

Samadhi (2017)
An immersive journey into the nature of consciousness and awakening. A beautiful complement to the deeper states of Reiki meditation and inner elemental alignment.

These video resources can be used for personal reflection, continuing education, Reiki classes, or seasonal workshops. They serve as powerful tools to **see, feel, and understand energy in motion**—and to remember the deeper story we're all a part of.

Just for today, I will let go of worry and trust the flow of life.

Message From The Author

The Five Elements are more than philosophical ideas — they are living energies that shape the world around us and move within us. Just like the seasons, we too cycle through phases of growth, release, stillness, joy, and reflection. What continues to amaze me about Reiki is how gracefully it mirrors these cycles — gently guiding energy back into flow where it has become stuck or forgotten.

When I began working with Reiki through the lens of elemental wisdom, everything deepened. Clients who were feeling overwhelmed in the summer found clarity by reconnecting with Fire. Those lost in grief during autumn softened as Metal helped them let go. Winter's stillness taught the beauty of rest and trust through Water, while Earth reminded us to ground and nourish. Wood called us to grow again.

The body is always speaking through these elemental imbalances — not just with pain or fatigue, but with emotions like worry, anger, fear, or the inability to move forward. Reiki doesn't just soothe the symptoms; it **translates the energy**, helping you understand where healing is needed and how to gently restore balance.

This book was born from my desire to give practitioners a more intuitive, nature-based map for healing — one that blends the structure of Traditional Chinese Medicine with the flow of Reiki energy. Whether you're working with others or walking your own healing path, I hope these teachings help you remember:

- You are connected.
- You are supported.
- You are part of something greater — and so is your healing.

Trust the rhythm.
Let the energy guide you.
And may you move through life with balance, grace, and wisdom.

With love and elemental light,
Dr. Constance Santego
Grand Reiki Master / Elemental Healing Educator

Just for today, I will let go of worry and trust the flow of life.

About The Author

Dream BIGGER!

Heal Beyond Time. Awaken Your Soul.

Dr. Constance Santego is a Grand Reiki Master, intuitive educator, and pioneer in energy-based healing. With over 25 years of experience as a practitioner and teacher in the holistic arts, she has empowered thousands of students to unlock their gifts, clear energetic blockages, and reconnect with the deeper purpose of their soul's journey.

Holding both a Ph.D. and a Doctorate in Natural Medicine, Dr. Santego bridges ancient healing traditions with modern metaphysical insight. Her approach combines energy medicine, spiritual psychology, and soul-based practices— creating powerful pathways for transformation at the physical, emotional, and karmic levels.

She is the founder of the **Reiki Wisdom** series, where Reiki becomes more than a healing tool—it becomes a lens for soul remembrance, ancestral release, and spiritual expansion. In her writings, Dr. Santego guides readers into previously unexplored territories of Reiki, offering tools for past life regression, ancestral clearing, and soul alignment.

In this volume, *Reiki and Karmic Healing*, she introduces a groundbreaking framework for karmic energy work— blending the "I Forgives" method, intuitive regression, Akashic Record access, and advanced Reiki techniques to support deep emotional release and soul-level freedom.

Dr. Santego is also the author of the *Nine Spiritual Gifts* novel series, where she brings teachings of soul contracts, reincarnation, and divine guidance to life through the journeys of Lexi and her companions. Each volume explores one of the nine gifts mentioned in 1 Corinthians 12, revealing how they awaken through spiritual practice and healing.

Across all her work, Dr. Santego holds true to one sacred truth:

Just for today, I will let go of worry and trust the flow of life.

"The deepest healing is not about fixing the past. It's about remembering who you really are—beyond time, beyond story, beyond pain."

She continues to write, teach, and mentor from her home in Alberta, Canada, where her work is devoted to helping others heal, awaken, and remember the light of their soul.

ALSO AVAILABLE

Play the game *Ikona* – Discover Your Inner Genie

For additional information on

Constance Santego's

wide range of Motivational Products, Coaching Sessions,
Spiritual Retreats,
Live Events and Educational Programs

Go to

www.ConstanceSantego.ca

Follow on Instagram - Constance_Santego and
Facebook - constancesantegoo

Subscribe and receive Free Information and Meditations on
my
YouTube Channel - Constance Santego

Just for today, I will let go of worry and trust the flow of life.

Just for today, I will let go of worry and trust the flow of life.

Just for today, I will let go of worry and trust the flow of life.

www.ingramcontent.com/pod-product-compliance
Lightning Source LLC
Chambersburg PA
CBHW070906120626
46546CB00001B/154